TILL
BETRAYAL
Do Us
PART

A Memoir of Surviving Narcissistic Abuse

CHERYL DYSON-BENNETT

Till Betrayal Do Us Part

© 2024 Cheryl Dyson-Bennett

All rights reserved. This book is printed in the United States of America. No part of this book may be used or reproduced in any form or by any means -electronic, mechanical, photocopy, recording, or otherwise - without written permission of the publisher, except in the case of brief quotations embodied in critical articles or reviews.

THE HOLY BIBLE, NEW INTERNATIONAL VERSION, NIV Copyright© 1973, 1978, 1984, 2011, by Biblica, Inc. Used by permission. All rights reserved worldwide.

Scriptures taken from the New King James Version. Copyright© 1982 by Thomas Nelson. Used with permission. All rights reserved.

Scripture quotations marked KJV are from the King James Version of the Bible.

Scripture quotations marked NLT are from the Holy Bible, New Living Translation, Copyright© 1996, 2004, 2007. Used by permission. All rights reserved.

Scripture quotations marked The Message are from The Message: The Bible in Contemporary English, Copyright© 1993, 1994, 1995, 2000, 2001, 2002. Used with permission. All rights reserved.

Designed for Greatness

Atlanta, Georgia

https://greatnesscoachingandconsulting.com/en-us/

Elevate Your Leadership Journey

CONTENTS

Acknowledgments v
Disclaimer ix
Prologue xiii

1   Journey Through Turmoil: The Shattered Facade Of Love 1
2   Embracing Sacrificial Love: Trials, Lessons, And A Quest
    For Freedom 17
3   Learning To Pray, Trust & Obey 23
4   Unforeseen Departures: Turmoil In Marriage 27
5   Trusting In Dreams: The Path To Forgiveness 39
6   Turmoil And Trials: The Unraveling Of Truth 53
7   The Fractured Truth: A Web Of Deception And Grief 65
8   Betrayal And Redemption 79
9   Revelations And Realizations: Uncovering The Truth 93
10 Embracing Change: Finding Home In Unexpected Places 101
11 Five Years Later 105

Conclusion 109
Soundtrack to My Journey 111
Appendix 115
Afterword 121
About the Author 123

ACKNOWLEDGMENTS

As I reflect on the journey that led to this book, I feel compelled to express my heartfelt gratitude for the opportunity to share my story—a story inspired by God for those navigating the challenging landscape of narcissistic abuse, just as I once did. This journey has been fraught with difficulties, yet it has also been rich with lessons that I hope will resonate with others on a similar path.

First and foremost, I want to thank God, the cornerstone of my life. As the older saints might say, He has been my guiding light and source of strength, lifting me from the depths of despair to a place of divine purpose. Through trials, tribulations, and profound heartbreak, I have discovered that healing and purpose often emerge from our most painful experiences. While I wouldn't wish for the pain, I endured on anyone, I am eternally grateful for the grace that saw me through. Jeremiah 29:11 assures me that God has plans for my life—plans for hope and a future. This promise empowers me to trust in His direction, no matter the challenges I face.

I extend my deepest appreciation to my family for their unwavering love and support. You have exemplified what it means to stand by one another, always showing up for me and my boys through thick and thin. Your prayers, phone calls, listening ears, and, most importantly, your love have made all the difference. I know the journey hasn't been easy, but your encouragement and faith in me have kept me looking forward to the incredible plans God has in store. He has continuously surprised me with His goodness.

To my beloved sons, I want to take a moment to express how deeply proud I am of you. Your courage, love, persistence, and determination have been awe-inspiring. Although our road has been challenging, you have navigated it with grace and strength. I couldn't have asked for better sons. As I've always told you, you are the light that shines in this world. No matter the challenges you face, always trust that God will see you through. Thank you for holding up my arms when I felt I didn't have the strength to do so myself. You have blessed me in countless ways, and I fervently pray that you will always remember who you are and whose you are. Past experiences do not define you—keep forging ahead and always put God first.

To my church leaders, thank you for standing in the gap through prayer and the powerful messages you deliver. Pastor Wilson, I am profoundly grateful for your friendship, mentorship, and guidance. For nearly 30 years, you have embodied the essence of a true friend and spiritual mother, always there to lift me up in faith.

A special shoutout to my sister from another mother, Ramona. You are more than just a friend; you are a prayer partner, life coach, and ministry leader. Your support has been invaluable, and I cherish our time together leading the Women of Destiny Empowerment Ministry. Your wisdom, compassion, and commitment to our shared mission inspire me daily. I look forward to continuing our work for the Lord and nurturing our beautiful friendship.

I also want to express my heartfelt gratitude to Rakera, my sister-in-Christ, who has been a steadfast support during difficult times. You have always been there to pray, fast, encourage, and listen—truly a friend to me. I could always count on your daily words of encouragement and your guidance through many challenges. I am forever grateful for you and the way God works through you in my life.

To Pastor Howard-John Wesley and the Alfred Street Baptist Church community, thank you for your commitment to your members and visitors alike. During my time there, I found true friendship and support that helped me navigate some of my darkest days. I want to especially recognize

Shanay, a sister I met in the Village in Waldorf, whose assistance and unwavering support during my separation and the sale of my home were invaluable. Your generosity and connections made a significant difference in my life.

Pastor Wesley, your sermons have been a lifeline for me, providing clarity and healing when I needed it most. I was deeply moved by messages like "Betrayed," "I Can't Believe You Did That to Me," and "Forgiving What You Can't Forget." These teachings helped me release the burdens that weighed me down and guided me toward a brighter future.

Lastly, I want to extend my deepest gratitude to Angee, my incredible editor. Your expertise, keen insights, and unwavering support have been instrumental in shaping this book. Thank you for your patience and guidance throughout the writing process, for believing in my story, and for helping me express it in the best possible way. I truly appreciate all the time and effort you invested in bringing this project to life.

I also want to take a moment to acknowledge my late husband. While our relationship was marked by challenges, I recognized the lessons I learned through our time together. Those experiences, though difficult, have played a significant role in shaping who I am today. I am grateful for the opportunity to grow and heal, finding strength in my journey toward understanding and self-empowerment.

To all who have walked this journey with me, thank you. Your love, encouragement, and unwavering belief in my story have been the wind beneath my wings. I hope that through these pages, you find hope, healing, and a sense of connection in your own journey.

DISCLAIMER

This memoir represents an honest and accurate account of the author's personal experiences and significant events from their life. While every effort has been made to convey the truth of these experiences, certain conversations and interactions have been reconstructed or elaborated upon to enhance narrative clarity and engagement. Additionally, to respect the privacy and confidentiality of individuals mentioned, some names and identifying details have been altered. The author has sought to balance the integrity of the recounting with the need to protect the identities of those involved.

This book delves deeply into personal experiences of narcissistic and emotional abuse. Readers should be aware that the content may evoke strong emotional responses and could act as a trigger for some individuals.

Triggers in this memoir may include, but are not limited to:

- **Detailed Descriptions of Emotional Manipulation**: Accounts of psychological tactics used to control, demean, or exploit others.
- **Narratives of Gaslighting**: Instances where the author describes being led to doubt their own perceptions or reality.
- **Explorations of Trauma and Psychological Distress**: Graphic depictions of the emotional impact and mental anguish resulting from abusive situations.
- **Recollections of Conflict and Betrayal**: Stories involving personal relationships strained or damaged by deceit and manipulation.

- **Reflections on Isolation and Helplessness**: Descriptions of feelings of being cut off from support networks or feeling powerless.

This memoir is intended to share personal insights and experiences with the hope of fostering understanding and support. However, if you are sensitive to these subjects or are currently navigating similar experiences, please proceed with caution. It is recommended that you seek support from mental health professionals or support groups if needed. Your well-being is of utmost importance, and self-care is crucial when engaging with potentially distressing content.

"What Happens When Love Turns Toxic?"

"In Till Betrayal Do Us Part, the author takes readers on a harrowing journey through the dark depths of narcissistic abuse, revealing the intricate web of manipulation that can hide behind a façade of love. With heart-wrenching honesty, she uncovers the emotional turmoil and confusion of living with a narcissist, all while discovering an unbreakable spirit within herself. This memoir is not just a story of survival; it's a powerful testament to resilience and healing, offering hope and empowerment to anyone seeking to reclaim their life. Through her struggles and triumphs, she proves that even in the darkest moments, there is a path to light and liberation."

QR- Mental Health Advocate

PROLOGUE

BETRAYAL: the act of deceiving someone or the fact of being betrayed: violation of a person's trust or confidence, of a moral standard, etc.

Betrayal is not merely an act of disloyalty; it pierces deep into the heart of trust, leaving behind fractured emotions and profound disillusionment. When someone we depend on breaches that trust—whether through deceit, moral violations, or outright infidelity—it triggers overwhelming emotions. The experience of betrayal propels individuals through feelings of sadness, anger, confusion, and a profound sense of disbelief.

In my own journey through betrayal, I have come to understand that its impact extends far beyond the initial breach of trust. It initiates a complex emotional process characterized by stages of grief and healing. This book is not merely a recounting of my personal triumph over <u>betrayal inflicted by narcissistic abuse</u>; it is a narrative intended to resonate deeply with readers who have navigated similar storms.

I have learned that healing from betrayal is a multifaceted journey. It demands confronting painful truths, reclaiming personal boundaries, and rebuilding a foundation of trust—both in oneself and in others. By exploring the intricacies of my own path to healing, I hope to offer companionship and solidarity to those who have weathered the devastating effects of betrayal.

Confronting my husband about his increasingly frequent late-night absences was like stepping into a nightmare. Each time he stumbled through the door at dawn, his silence was more deafening than any words he could have spoken. One morning, around 8 am, he returned home as if nothing was amiss, brushing past me with a cold indifference that cut deep. "Where have you been?" I demanded, my voice trembling with a mix of anger and hurt. He didn't even acknowledge my presence, heading straight to bed without a single word. The dismissiveness infuriated me; it was a stark reminder of how little my concerns mattered to him.

But it wasn't just one isolated incident. Another time, on what was supposed to be a family day out, he vanished again, returning only after I had packed my bags in frustration, ready to spend a night away at a hotel. The bitter realization struck me as I circled aimlessly in the car: he had someone pick him up the moment I left. It was as if my feelings held no weight, no significance compared to his own desires. The betrayal stung; there was no empathy, only his selfish pursuit of pleasure, regardless of the pain he caused.

Even when we managed to venture out together as a family, his demeanor was telling. He'd be lethargic, constantly checking the time, rushing us through outings that were meant to be cherished moments. Yet, when it came to his own pursuits, suddenly, he had boundless energy and enthusiasm. It was a cruel double standard that left me questioning where I stood in his priorities.

Months later, the truth of his infidelity came crashing down around me like a tidal wave. I found myself in the doctor's office repeatedly, grappling with UTIs that seemed to have no medical explanation. Confronting him, I struggled to keep my voice steady, asking if he had been unfaithful. His denial was swift, almost rehearsed, cutting through me like a knife. But the signs were there, in the distance that had grown between us, and in the physical toll his actions had taken on my health.

Our intimacy had become strained long before I found out the truth. When we were together, it was clear his focus was elsewhere, his touch devoid of the warmth and connection I craved. The last time we made love, it was a hollow act, leaving me in tears afterward, overwhelmed by the sense of betrayal that lingered in the air. There was a strange scent, unfamiliar and unsettling, confirming what my heart had already feared.

In each of these moments, the pain of betrayal cut deeper than any words could convey. His actions spoke volumes, shredding the trust that had once been the foundation of our marriage. It was a betrayal that went beyond mere words or actions—it shattered my sense of security, leaving me to question everything I thought I knew about love and commitment.

As a result of his betrayal, I was set on a terrible course, navigating through stages of betrayal trauma — a complex and deeply personal journey.

On the next several pages, I outline for you each stage and the emotions that accompany each one.

STAGE 1 — SHOCK

The initial stage of betrayal is characterized by shock—a visceral reaction akin to a physical blow upon discovering the betrayal. It is a phase of disbelief and numbness, where the mind struggles to comprehend the reality of what has transpired.

STAGE 2 — DISBELIEF/DENIAL

Following the shock, disbelief and denial often set in. There is a natural resistance to accepting the painful truth as the mind attempts to shield itself from the full emotional impact. Questions arise, doubts linger, and hope persists that the betrayal is a misunderstanding or a dreadful dream.

STAGE 3 — OBSESSION

As the reality of betrayal sinks in, obsession takes hold. There is an intense fixation on uncovering every detail, replaying events, and searching relentlessly for answers. This phase is marked by a desperate need to make sense of the incomprehensible.

STAGE 4 — ANGER/SADNESS

Acceptance brings forth a torrent of emotions, primarily anger and profound sadness. There is mourning not only for the loss of trust and security but also for the shattered ideals of the relationship. Anger may be directed towards the betrayer or inwardly towards oneself for being blindsided. Sadness permeates thoughts as the loss of what was believed to be true becomes painfully evident.

STAGE 5 — BARGAINING

In an attempt to regain control and mitigate pain, bargaining ensues. There may be excuses made for the betrayer's actions, efforts to rationalize or minimize the betrayal. This phase involves negotiating with oneself or with a higher power, seeking ways to undo the damage inflicted.

STAGE 6 MOURNING

The mourning stage is characterized by deep sorrow and withdrawal. Interest in once-enjoyed activities wanes, and social interactions diminish. It is a period of introspection and profound sadness as one comes to terms with shattered expectations and dreams.

STAGE 7 ACCEPTANCE/RECOVERY

Acceptance does not imply condoning the betrayal; rather, it signifies coming to terms with a new reality and envisioning a future beyond the pain. Recovery is a gradual process marked by self-discovery, self-compassion, and renewed resilience. It involves rebuilding trust in oneself and others, finding closure, and moving forward with life.

Navigating the stages of betrayal is a deeply personal journey, complex and arduous. Seeking support from trusted friends, family, or professionals is crucial to navigating the emotional challenges and emerging stronger from the experience.

This book is all about the strength of the human spirit in the face of profound betrayal. It is a beacon of hope for those seeking to reclaim their sense of self-worth and trust after enduring the storm. Through shared experiences and insights, may it illuminate paths toward healing and renewal.

1

JOURNEY THROUGH TURMOIL: THE SHATTERED FACADE OF LOVE

September 21, 2019, marked a significant day in my life – one bursting with anticipation and excitement. It was the day I headed on my first journey out of town to promote my latest book, *In the Arms of Jesus: Favor, Increase, and Promotion*. I had practiced my speech on the theme of "Selflessness," a topic close to my heart as I believed my own experiences epitomized its meaning. Through my life, I had learned the value of putting others before myself, a lesson I was eager to share with others.

However, the morning of that pivotal day took an unexpected turn. As I busied myself with preparations, I noticed an empty seat at the breakfast table. My husband, who was usually first to eat, was missing. That struck me as odd. His subsequent entrance into our bedroom with a somber expression only added to my confusion. Instead of words of encouragement or support for my event, he uttered a request that left me stunned - a request that threatened to change my family forever. He wanted me to make a list of how I would like matters handled if we were considering separation.

Perplexed and taken aback, I struggled to understand this odd proposal. I ignored his persistence and continued with my preparations, hoping it was just a passing whim and he was just in another of his strange moods of late. Yet, his insistence forced me to acknowledge the seriousness of the situation. Reluctantly, I complied with his request, expressing my disagreement with the notion of separation. I made the list my way as I wrote, "I am not in agreement with a separation; thus, I do not have a list."

As I drove to the event, my mind buzzed with questions about the sudden rift in our relationship. This was not the day for such big emotions. I needed all my energies focused on the major events I was about to attend and speak at. But how could I ignore such an earth-shattering request from the man I pledged my life to? It wasn't until later that I connected the dots to a significant event that had shaken my husband's world months earlier – his unexpected firing from a job he had dedicated years to. The memory of that fateful day flooded back, bringing with it a sense of unease and uncertainty about the future.

The memory of the day my husband lost his job is still vivid in my mind. I was at work when a call came from one of his colleagues, alerting me to a situation at his workplace. According to him, there were whispers about my husband being summoned to the manager's office. While it sounded like he had been let go, nothing was certain as his phone went straight to voicemail when the colleague tried to reach him.

My heart sank upon hearing this. I dialed my husband's office number, only to hear his boss's voice on the other end. Without saying a word, I ended the call abruptly. A sense of foreboding washed over me, prompting me to leave work immediately and head home. On the way, I attempted to call my husband's cell again. This time, he answered, informing me he was on his way back. When he arrived, his demeanor was subdued as he revealed the news of his dismissal. I did my best to comfort him, assuring him that we would get through this together.

In the weeks following his dismissal, my husband embarked on a job hunt within his field. During this time, he expressed to me that he held me responsible for his struggles in finding employment. I found it perplexing, as I couldn't comprehend how I could be at fault. I believed his frustrations were being unfairly directed towards me, perhaps as a result of his anger and disappointment.

Despite his misdirected blame, I remained steadfast in my support for him. In fact, I proposed a potential solution: the establishment of his own HVAC business. Given his extensive expertise and experience in the field, it seemed like a logical step forward. I helped him devise a comprehensive plan, from outlining the services he would offer to acquiring the necessary tools and equipment. We even brainstormed potential business names, ultimately settling on Bennett HVAC 360, a name that reflected both professionalism and completeness in service provision.

I took an active role in kickstarting the business, organizing marketing strategies, designing logos, and crafting promotional materials. While I dedicated myself to laying the groundwork for Bennett HVAC 360, my

Narcissistic Rage

Narcissistic Rage: Narcissistic rage is common for those with NPD as they grow increasingly angry with any display of vulnerability. This anger can be triggered when they are "called out," their image has been damaged, or their shortcomings or wrongdoings are highlighted. The narcissist will use this rage to deflect from and overshadow the true issues.

A narcissist can become easily enraged if a setback occurs in their life, job, or relationship. Not getting their way results in both a loss of control and a bruised ego. In these situations, they may lash out with rage to either deflect from the conflict or regain a sense of authority.

They feel a loss of control

If the narcissist feels like they are losing control of the situation, a rage fit allows them to regain power over those around them. Even if they are receiving unfavorable reactions from their targets, the narcissist revels in the attention and superiority they have restored.

husband managed to secure some temporary side work while awaiting news of full-time employment opportunities.

During this period of my husband's temporary, unfortunate unemployment, two of our four children were enrolled in college. As they prepared to go back for the new semesters to their two universities located three hours away from each other, my husband decided not to join us. Consequently, the remaining two sons and I had to travel together to take the other two back to their respective colleges. I was disheartened that my husband didn't go, but I assumed his low spirits were due to his recent job loss and the financial strain it had placed on our family.

With the new semester underway, tuition became a growing concern. Our children were ineligible for grants because our prior income and loans made it appear that we were capable of covering their tuition. This financial burden was ours to bear as a single income family. Though I was still employed full-time, we had other monthly obligations. The financial strain put immense tension on our marriage. He felt unworthy and helpless without a job.

His temper was easily triggered, and the slightest thing would set him off. His irritability and agitation were at an unprecedented level. His behavior got worse as he began to excessively consume alcohol and use recreational drugs. Taking notice of these changes, eventually, I asked him if he was involved in any prohibited activities. He replied with rage, saying, "If I was, I wouldn't be penniless." Still, despite his protests, it was clear that something was wrong; I could sense it in my spirit.

My suspicions were piqued when my husband suddenly announced a trip to Miami, claiming he wanted to visit someone he hadn't seen in a while. The timing couldn't have been worse, considering our precarious financial situation. The expenses of such a trip were definitely not accounted for in our budget. I felt not only frustrated by his decision to go but also worried about who he was meeting. This person had a shady past, and I wasn't sure if they had truly left behind their illicit activities.

This trip wasn't an isolated incident; my husband embarked on several other journeys afterward, none of which he consulted me about or invited me to join. On one occasion, he even had a "friend" accompany him, but when I tried to inquire about it, he dodged the questions and refused to provide any details. The lack of transparency and inclusion in his decisions left me feeling uneasy and unsettled.

After a stretch of unemployment, my husband finally caught a break. Another HVAC company offered him a full-time position, complete with the perk of a company vehicle. He was over the moon about the news and suddenly became more attentive to our relationship. We marked the occasion with a special date night, a much-needed break from the constant worry and stress that had plagued us for so long.

> **Narcissistic Injury**
>
> A Narcissistic injury occurs when a narcissist thinks their self-esteem or self-worth is threatened. Because narcissists have exceptionally low self-esteem, they become incredibly defensive and frustrated when their shortcomings are pointed out. Thus, the distress associated with their false self being exposed can result in narcissistic rage.
>
> Narcissistic rage can lead to negative impacts such as financial challenges. Narcissists can be impulsive when in a fit of rage and may engage in gambling or overspending.
>
> There might be difficulties maintaining employment: If a narcissist can't control their rage in the workplace, their behavior is both unprofessional and a liability. Ultimately, frequent outbursts can lead to job loss.

Walking along the Marina, soaking in the serene views, felt like a balm for our weary souls. Despite the pleasant atmosphere, I couldn't shake the feeling that something was amiss with my husband. When I suggested taking a picture together to capture the moment, his mood noticeably soured. He quickly insisted that I refrain from posting it on Facebook.

His reaction caught me off guard, and I must have shown my surprise because he swiftly backtracked, telling me I could post it if I wanted to. This sudden change in demeanor left me feeling uneasy, as if there were underlying issues that hadn't been addressed. *Why doesn't he want me to post our picture on Facebook? We are a married couple. Is he ashamed of me?* I didn't want to fight and chose not to post the picture. Even though we were on a celebratory outing, his demeanor gave me the impression that he did not want to be there and didn't want others to see us behaving as a couple.

> **Silent Treatment**
>
> This tactic is typically employed by people with narcissistic tendencies. It is designed to (1) place the abuser in a position of control; (2) silence the target's attempts at assertion; (3) avoid conflict resolution/personal responsibility/compromise; or (4) punish the target for a perceived ego slight. Often, the result of the silent treatment is exactly what the person with narcissism wishes to create: a reaction from the target and a sense of control.
>
> Narcissists may use the silent treatment to communicate they are unhappy with you, to control you, or as a form of punishment. If the narcissist uses the silent treatment to deflect responsibility for something they have done wrong, it can also be a form of narcissistic gaslighting

My husband's behavior the following week was unusually reticent. What was even more peculiar was that he had started to voluntarily do chores around the house. He had never offered to help in the past and usually refused any household duties. These tasks were mundane to him. Yet, there he was washing and folding clothes, tidying up, and handling minor issues in the house. He behaved like a completely different person. On the other hand, he was aloof, giving me silent treatment.

Being on the receiving end of his silent treatment, I wanted to do something to break the tension. One night in bed, I tried to draw him in for an embrace to show my love and affection, but he rejected it. I turned away, hurt by even more confirmation that something was amiss. My woman's intuition didn't fail.

As I reflected on the trials and tribulations of my marriage, I couldn't help but delve deeper into our past. The strain in our relationship had been present long before my husband's job loss. Despite my fervent prayers for our union's well-being, this year felt particularly desolate and isolating.

Our connection had dwindled into more of a functional partnership than a passionate relationship. We seemed to only convene to manage household expenses and discuss matters concerning our children. Meanwhile, my husband seemed to wander wherever his desires led him, seldom returning home. His absence left me in a perpetual state of uncertainty; I often had no idea of his whereabouts—whether he was gambling, shooting pool, or simply lingering anywhere but home.

> **Stonewalling**
>
> Stonewalling is a communication behavior that is characterized by refusing to engage in or respond to a conversation or a person's attempts to communicate.
>
> Stonewalling is a metaphor that draws from the concept of building a stone wall that does not allow for connection.
>
> Stonewalling is a tactic that involves withdrawing from communication and deliberately avoiding providing any information, feedback, or emotional response, effectively shutting down a conversation or interaction.
>
> This can include completely ignoring another person, physically turning away from someone, and/ or engaging in another activity to avoid interaction.

Even when he was physically present, he seemed emotionally distant, preoccupied with his phone and conversations with others. His habit of staying out late, sometimes for days at a time, filled me with worry and desperation. Despite my attempts to reach out, my calls went unanswered, overshadowed by his constant engagement with his phone.

His increasingly secretive behavior around his mobile device did not escape my notice. He took it with him everywhere, even to the bathroom or shower, as if its presence needed to be constantly monitored. When I broached the subject and requested to see his phone, he adamantly refused, going as far as to install additional security measures and physically blocking my attempts to access it like smacking my hand away if I tried to touch it. This growing distance and secrecy only fueled my apprehension and sense of unease about the state of our marriage.

He hadn't always been so secretive. In the past, I always knew his phone's password; he had nothing to conceal. As time progressed, there was a shift in his behavior that signaled something sinister was afoot.

Communication was not a significant part of his nature; it was unidirectional, with me doing the majority of the talking. He had become withdrawn, not having to respond to me or take responsibility for his actions. His lack of interaction meant he did not have to address or take accountability of his behavior, further deepening the emotional distance between us. His reluctance to communicate effectively left me feeling isolated and frustrated, as he evaded any meaningful discussion or accountability.

> **Double Life of Narcissists**
>
> Narcissists are known for their lack of empathy, sense of entitlement, and their tendency to exploit and manipulate others for their own gain. One of the ways they do this is by engaging in a behavior known as "ghosting," where they suddenly disappear. This can leave their spouse in a state of utter confusion, asking why or wondering what they did wrong to make the narcissist build a second life.

I wept to God countless times, imploring Him, and searching for His presence to repair what was broken in my marriage. I pleaded for our marriage and felt God wasn't listening. I even dared to ask God if He was concerned about me and what I was going through, and if He would alter my husband's heart. I desired my husband to be the man of God I knew he was capable of being. I wanted him to be a loving father to his children. I wanted him to be a loving spouse to me. He said he loved me, but his actions did not match those words.

I was left with the aching hole of loneliness accompanied by endless questions: Why did he have to go out all the time? Why wouldn't he respect me? Why did he forsake his family? Why did he refuse to communicate with me?

It was true that he was a classic introvert, but he had no problems talking to others. He was there for his friends, extended family, colleagues, etc., doing whatever they asked. I desperately wanted him to show that same level of enthusiasm toward his family. Instead, we received the least amount. He gave all of himself to the world, playing the role of the ideal husband and father. If only they knew what we had to endure behind closed doors.

Not only was I dealing with his silent treatment, but I also found myself enduring numerous instances of disrespect that made me yearn for the times when my husband simply ignored me. One notable incident occurred in August when he insisted, we host a gathering for some of his longtime friends. I prepared a meal, welcomed them into our home, and engaged in conversation over food. While they were pleasant company, I couldn't help but feel like I didn't belong in their world.

> **R-E-S-P-E-C-T**
>
> Narcissists often show blatant disrespect to their spouses through open flirtation with other women, using it as a tactic to boost their own ego and assert dominance. This behavior undermines the spouse's sense of security and self-worth, creating feelings of jealousy and inadequacy. It serves to reinforce the narcissist's control while publicly devaluing their partner, deepening the emotional harm and instability in the relationship.

Unlike them, I didn't subscribe to the latest trends or have a taste for luxury brands. I didn't partake in the competitive social scene they seemed to thrive in. Instead, I lived a modest life guided by principles of integrity and simplicity, untouched by the allure of worldly possessions. However, my husband appeared determined to portray himself as the epitome of success and influence. He constantly sought to assert his dominance, to be the center of attention, admired, and depended upon by others. This misalignment in values and priorities left me feeling increasingly out of place in my own home.

The unmistakable infatuation my husband displayed towards his friend's wife was impossible to ignore. His gaze lingered on her, devoid of any attempt at subtlety. If it wasn't for the fact that his eyes were betraying me, I could understand the attraction. She exuded beauty, draped in designer attire, captivating everyone's attention. Throughout the passing hours of the party, my husband remained fixated on her, his interest palpable even as she and her husband prepared to leave.

Confronting him about his behavior later, I was met with a dismissive response: "I am a man." His casual justification left me incredulous. How could he be so callous and insensitive, openly displaying his attraction to another woman without regard for my feelings or the impact it would have on our relationship? It was a painful reminder of the growing chasm between us and the disregard he showed for our bond.

Weeks later, we made our way to New Jersey for a couple of events. Our first stop was the *Unstoppable You Conference*, which I attended to support a friend who was the mastermind of the organization. I was a special guest on a podcast with one of the keynote speakers of the conference. The event was exceptional, but this did not stop my husband from glancing at other women while in my presence. What was the matter with this man? Why did he seem to show interest in females while being with me?

The evening took a disconcerting turn when my husband's behavior became increasingly erratic at an engagement party we attended just four hours later. His actions towards me seemed uncharacteristically inappropriate, leaving others to take notice of his conduct. Amidst the social gathering, several individuals approached me, expressing interest in purchasing copies of my book after hearing about it. My husband, seemingly supportive, hurried to retrieve copies from the car for them to buy. However, when it was time to leave, he abruptly left me behind, rushing out the door without a second thought.

Having arranged for us to stay in Atlantic City for the night, anticipating the long day ahead, I had hoped for a peaceful evening after the event.

However, upon checking into our hotel room, my husband's demeanor shifted once again, this time filled with an inexplicable enthusiasm. He hastily made his way to the hotel's casino and spent the entire night gambling, leaving me alone with our children in the room. Sadly, this scenario had become all too familiar—a stark reminder of the increasing frequency with which I found myself alone without him.

In the midst of my tumultuous marriage and personal struggles, I felt a divine calling from the Lord urging me to write a book. This message was reaffirmed by the guidance of numerous religious figures. Initially, I began writing a devotional, but as I continued to seek the Lord's direction, I realized He wanted me to delve deeper into my own relational hardships and how He sustained me through them, even during moments when His presence felt distant.

Though initially hesitant and anxious about fulfilling this calling, I eventually surrendered to God's will and embarked on the challenging journey of writing the book He had laid on my heart. Recognizing my need for guidance and support, I sought the assistance of a book-writing mentor and enrolled in a writing course to hone my skills. I wanted it to be the best it could be so that people in situations like me would be drawn to it and relate to it.

With my focus redirected towards this endeavor, I found solace and purpose in pouring my heart and soul into the pages of my testimony, easing the pain of my husband's betrayal. Despite the difficulties and uncertainties surrounding my broken marriage, the words flowed effortlessly as I recounted my personal journey of faith and resilience. Through this process, I discovered a newfound sense of empowerment and fulfillment as I embraced my calling to share my story with others. I completed and published *In the Arms of Jesus*, a book of healing and deliverance.

In the Arms of Jesus became a true testimony of my life and the gifts of love and faithfulness shone through. The book takes the reader on a journey through my missteps and the unbelievable fortitude I had to develop to recuperate from them. Many remarked they observed a young lady with great strength seeking her fantasy life as she confronted pregnancies and bolstered a beau while they both battled with the errant decisions they made. My story accentuates the intensity of trust even amid disappointment and errors. *In the Arms of Jesus* is a declaration of a youthful lady who, at long last, comprehends absolution and benevolence from her Savior, Jesus Christ, as she offers a similar degree of pardoning to the young man who becomes her spouse.

After completing the book, I asked my husband to inspect it for his consent as he was unaware of certain details I had included. I repeatedly encouraged him to read the manuscript. Upon completing it, he became angry to learn that I had been involved with someone else during a time we were not together. I was puzzled by his reaction since he and I lived in two different states at the time. He quizzed me about it, and I honestly told him everything; I had nothing to hide. He became even more infuriated upon learning the details even though he and I weren't together at that point.

My husband requested that I call the guy (a man he happened to know), which I did. When the guy answered the phone, my husband told the man that he didn't want him to talk to me, and said he knew how all this worked as he had been around. I was puzzled by his behavior because I had no current association with this man and hadn't talked to the man in an incredibly long time. We would chat, at the most, twice a year. Each time I talked to the guy, my husband was a part of our conversation since he knew him. I had concealed nothing from him. But his anger reached a level where he called other people and made it known to them. He behaved as if I had been unfaithful when that was far from the truth, leaving me longing for the days when we were unified as a couple.

After the release of my book, I noticed a shift in my husband's attitude towards my work. He began to openly express pride in my accomplishments, passionately promoting the book to his associates and friends. He even went above and beyond by purchasing copies to distribute to others and sharing a heartfelt review on social media.

As the book gained traction and sold copies, it garnered a mixed response from readers. Many resonated deeply with the content, finding solace in its relatable themes, while others were drawn in by the more sensational aspects. However, when members of my husband's inner circle read the book, their reactions were notably different. Some harshly criticized it, claiming it painted an unrealistic picture of our relationship.

This criticism deeply offended my husband, leading him to feel unjustly judged because of the book's portrayal of our story. Despite his discomfort, the book remained a faithful representation of our journey. It was never meant to expose or sensationalize but rather to offer a narrative of inspiration, hope, and redemption to those who might find themselves in similar circumstances.

These memories might have been factors leading to my husband's desire to end our marriage. It's left me pondering how someone can profess love yet fail to demonstrate it in their actions. Genuine love is patient and kind; it doesn't envy or brag, nor is it arrogant or rude. It doesn't demand its own way and is not easily angered, nor does it rejoice in wrongdoing. Love bears all, believes all, hopes all, and endures all **(1 Corinthians 13:4-7)**. True love would never condone a husband treating his wife with anything other than love and respect.

Reflecting on past memories, I recalled a time when my husband was away on a week-long business trip to New York. Initially, we stayed in touch regularly for the first two days, but communication dwindled from day 3 to 5. Then, out of the blue, he called one day and asked for a picture of me. It struck me as odd yet strangely gratifying, as I interpreted it as a sign of his longing for me. After all, what woman wouldn't want to feel desired by her partner?

However, upon his return home, his behavior took a perplexing turn. He seemed distant and disinterested in intimacy, avoiding me at every opportunity. I was left feeling rejected and confused, unable to understand what had changed. Despite my obvious distress, he remained indifferent to my feelings, adding to my sense of insecurity and self-doubt.

A few nights later, I was rummaging through what we referred to as our junk drawer. In it, I found clinical results from an urgent care facility. The paperwork showed his name, the examination date, and the tests performed with the outcome of each. He was examined shortly after his trip to New York for STDs! What? Instantly, I seized the results and asked him about it. He asked me to grab my Bible as he explained.

> **Narcissistic Addiction**
>
> One of the common Narcissist addictions is sex. The others are gambling, drugs, and alcohol

His tale went like this: he was at a bar during his business trip. While at the bar, drinking heavily and smoking marijuana, he became inebriated and ended up sleeping with someone he met there. I didn't know if I should slap him, yell obscenities, or kick him. Instead, I fell to the ground and started to bawl. How could this be? I questioned him as I attempted to regain composure, bombarding him with a plethora of questions: "How could you engage in intimacy with a total stranger? Does our marriage mean anything to you? Why would you break our vows? Did you not take precautions? How could you have sex with a stranger, and you and I can go weeks without sexual intercourse? Is the individual a stranger? Is it somebody from your past?"

Discovering that the man I once called my spouse had been unfaithful and potentially exposed us to a sexually transmitted disease was beyond painful—it was nauseating. I couldn't help but wonder whatever happened to the idea of husbands honoring their wives and treating them with kindness, as we're instructed to do when living together. The Bible teaches that, while a wife may be considered weaker in some respects, she is nonetheless an equal partner in God's blessing of new life. This betrayal shattered my trust and left me grappling with the devastating consequences of infidelity. Appreciate her as you should so your prayers will not be hindered **(1 Peter 3:7)**. In simpler words, "You shall not commit adultery **(Exodus 20:14).**

I yearned for my partner to love me; why was it so hard to love me like I loved him? This shook me profoundly. A notable expression says we cannot truly have our cake and eat it. But that is what he did. He wanted all the advantages of a relationship without devotion.

2

EMBRACING SACRIFICIAL LOVE: TRIALS, LESSONS, AND A QUEST FOR FREEDOM

Stepping into the Authors Café in Philadelphia, I made a concerted effort to maintain composure, my emotions tightly in check. I was there with a purpose, a mission laid upon my heart. With a silent prayer to God for clarity and guidance, I surrendered to His will, trusting in His divine plan.

As I prepared to address the audience, my scripted words took on a new resonance, infused with a sense of sacrificial love. Rather than speaking from a place of mere knowledge and understanding, I found myself drawing from a deeper wellspring of compassion and empathy. It was as if God's presence enveloped me, guiding my words and intentions with grace and purpose.

Sacrificial love occurs when someone loves with all their heart, takes action based on that love, and doesn't think solely about themselves.

This type of love is modeled for us by God. According to **1 John 3:16-18**, "We can recognize true love because of what Jesus did for us. He gave his life for us, and we should be willing to give our lives for our brothers. If someone has enough to live on, but a brother or sister is in need, and they refuse to help—how can they claim to love God? Little children, our love should not just be words. We must show the truth by our actions" (NIV).

Sacrificial love in a relationship happens when we choose to respect and appreciate the other's feelings and take their emotions into account as if they were our own. We learn to find pride and joy in loving them. As **1 John 4:12** says, "No one has ever seen God. But if we love each other, God lives in us, and his love is made complete in us" **(NIV)**.

A preacher once said, "If you yearn for your partner to be more loving, then you should demonstrate more love. If you want your mate to pray more, then you should pray more." Sacrificial love is equated to the saying in **Luke 6:31**, "Do to others as you would have them do to you" **(NIV)**. A more thorough interpretation of self-sacrificing love can be found in **1 Corinthians 13:4**: "Love is patient, gentle, and generous. It has no envy; it does not boast; it is not proud. It does not dishonor others; it does not seek its own interests; it is not easily angered; it does not recall wrongs. Love does not rejoice in evil but rejoices with the truth. It always protects, always believes, always hopes, and always perseveres. Love never fails."

God has revealed his love to us through Jesus Christ: "This is how God showed his love among us: He sent his one and only Son into the world that we might live through him. This is love: not that we loved God, but that he loved us and sent his Son as an atoning sacrifice for our sins" (**1 John 4:9-10**). Jesus is our example of how to love. And while self-sacrificing love can be hard to practice, God guides us in loving others just as He does. As Jesus said about the greatest commandments, "You shall love the Lord your God with all your heart and with all your soul and with all your mind and with all your strength.' The second is this: 'You shall love your neighbor as yourself.' There is no other commandment greater than these" (**Mark 12:30-31**). Placing God first will help us love as Jesus loved – selflessly.

This message served as a profound declaration of my life and the deep affection I harbored for my husband. It encapsulated the selfless love that endured through every joy and sorrow, navigating the highs and lows of our journey together. Rooted in the unconditional love of God, my affection for him transcended any wrongdoing, as forgiveness had already been granted for any past transgressions. I pondered **Matthew 6:14-15**, "If you forgive the offenses of men, your heavenly Father will also forgive you, but if you do not forgive the offenses of men, neither will your Father forgive your offenses."

Forgiving my husband for his multitude of mistakes was a challenging journey, one that I couldn't have navigated without the grace of God. As the evening portion of the book event drew to a close, I found solace in the shared stories of many women who resonated with my experiences and thanked me for my openness.

Despite the sense of accomplishment, I felt in connecting with others and offering support, there lingered a heavy weight of failure in my marriage. It was a bittersweet realization, acknowledging the strides I had made in personal growth while grappling with the painful reality of a relationship in turmoil.

On the ride home, I thought back on how I had relentlessly prayed for my husband and our marriage. Numerous times, I knelt at the Lord's feet, praying, trusting, and believing Him for a marriage made in heaven, a perfect marriage. I always prayed and fasted for my husband and recently went on a *"30-day Pray for Your Spouse Fast."*

Each recitation was a heartfelt plea to the divine, a reaffirmation of my belief in God's ability to intervene and bring about positive change. It was a source of comfort and empowerment, knowing that I was actively contributing to the betterment of my husband's circumstances through the power of prayer. I wrote out affirmations and said them out loud with faith and assurance that God would bring about a change in my husband's situation. Reciting these supplications to God was my way of affirming this.

- ❖ That he lives by God's plan for his life (Ephesians 4:1-2)
- ❖ That he would continue to lead, and that God would be glorified in our marriage (Ephesians 5:25-29)
- ❖ That the Lord would bless the work of his work (Proverbs 22:29)
- ❖ That he would lean on Christ in his trials (Psalm 46:1)
- ❖ His integrity (Proverbs 11:3)
- ❖ His temptations (1 Corinthians 10:13)
- ❖ That he would have a giving heart (Proverbs 28:27)
- ❖ For discernment in handling finances (Luke 16:13)
- ❖ That he would trust in God's plan, not his own (Jeremiah 29:11)
- ❖ That he would give everything to the Lord in prayer (1 Thessalonians 5:17)
- ❖ That he would seek wisdom (James 1:5)
- ❖ That God would provide him with discernment (Philippians 1:9-10)
- ❖ That the Lord would teach him how to be a good husband and likewise me a good wife (Ephesians 5:22-23)
- ❖ That he would submit his fears to God (Psalms 118:6)
- ❖ That he would fully grasp his purpose in Christ (Romans 8:28)
- ❖ For his health (1 Corinthians 6:12)
- ❖ For his strength (Psalm 28:7)
- ❖ That he would be surrounded by people who bring him up (Proverbs 13:20)
- ❖ That he would boldly declare the Truth of the Gospel (Acts 28:31)
- ❖ That he would grow spiritually through reading, studying, and prayer (2 Peter 3:18)
- ❖ That he would have a humble, teachable spirit (Proverbs 15:33)
- ❖ That he would be full of patience and peace (Romans 14:19)
- ❖ His heart (Proverbs 4:23)
- ❖ His future (Psalm 119:105)

Despite my fervent prayers, I couldn't shake the worry that God remained silent to my pleas and petitions. Were my cries unheard? Was this my moment of despair? The story of the Israelites weighed heavily on my mind—their long years of slavery under Pharaoh's rule, enduring cruel treatment and oppression. It took the appointment of Moses as their advocate to confront Pharaoh, the formidable obstacle standing between them and freedom. Like the Israelites, I felt trapped, facing my own formidable barriers to liberation.

Was my husband the Pharaoh of my life? I understood that Pharaoh symbolized "anyone" or "anything" that obstructs us from being free for God in the present. Was I going through a pruning process? John 15:1-2, Jesus says, "Every branch in Me that does not bear fruit, He takes away; and every branch that continues to bear fruit, He [repeatedly] prunes, so that it will bear more fruit [even richer and finer fruit]." Pruning is crucial for us to grow in our journey with God.

I needed to ask myself: Was I lugging those "lifeless branches" in my life? Could it be that my marriage was no longer serving God's purpose or benefiting either of us? The harsh reality is that carrying around dead weight can lead to misery. Sometimes, we must endure the pain of allowing God to prune away the parts of us that no longer bear fruit.

3

LEARNING TO PRAY, TRUST & OBEY

Throughout that year, my concerns felt endless, and I struggled to confide in others about what I was going through. Instead, I sought solace in journaling, where I encountered God daily. In those pages, I poured out my deepest feelings and emotions, finding God to be my closest friend and confidant. Despite moments when I felt distant from Him, I trusted in His presence and relied on His unwavering support.

In the stillness of those moments, I prayed earnestly, and as I communed with God, His voice became clear to me. His words offered reassurance, comfort, and guidance, especially during the challenging days of February when I questioned Him about my husband's situation. My prayers were heartfelt, seeking wisdom and understanding in the midst of uncertainty.

O Lord, I beseech Thee to make visible any situation concerning my husband. I am done with his shenanigans. I love him, yet no longer have strong emotions because he has caused me too much distress. Addressing Thee as a friend and a confidant, why must I continually put up with his immaturity while he reacts so adversely when I tease him? I strive to focus my concentration on Thee and away from him. There comes a moment when one has been through enough; he must either shift or be removed from my life. He can be egocentric and self-absorbed; he habitually keeps secrets from me, while I am open. O Lord, you know all and see all. Assist me, Lord. Am I delusional?

On April 6th, I implored God again for answers:

Gratefully, I thank you, Lord Jesus Christ, for this day. As I turn to You, Most High, I seek absolution for my transgressions. Refresh me, cleanse me, and make me whole. Almighty, why am I stuck on this tumultuous journey with my husband? Why? Is it me? I'm aware that I often come to You about him, and I'm cognizant that it might be tedious. In any case, Lord, You see. How is it okay for him to stay out all night and come back at 5 am like it's ordinary? Why do I have to be the one who always asks for forgiveness when half the time I'm not even in the wrong?

Lord, my mind is tired. I am physically depleted from fighting. Please intervene for my sanity. I know I am a conqueror through Christ who strengthens me, and the tricks and schemes of the enemy will not defeat me. Lord, I am asking you to relieve me of this emotional rollercoaster.

> **The Guessing Game**
>
> You're always guessing how not to trigger a narcissist. You're damned if you do and you're damned if you don't do something ... and these people are impossible to keep happy, because they're not happy on the inside.

Why Lord? Do you not understand that I am tired of this? Why can't I have the love I desire I want to feel appreciated, not just for a moment. I want to feel free to be myself. Not to walk on eggshells. I want to experience life together. I want to travel. I don't want to live two separate lives, feeling like it's a contractual relationship, not a covenant one. I want to feel like I'm in a union and not a business deal. I don't want my spouse staying out all night unless it's with me. I don't want him going to any establishments that are of disgrace. I want someone to grow old together with. Nice strolls in the park or a carriage ride. I want much more for myself. I have given this man 25 years of my life where I have been there through thick and thin. But for what? Lord, am I selfish? Do I expect too much? Am I not your daughter?

> **Devaluation**
>
> Narcissists are takers and attach themselves to givers. They reduce the marriage relationship to that of roommates or business partners, causing their spouses to compete for loyalty and attention

Since I am of royalty, I should be treated as such. I will not settle for less than what you have for me. I want a God-fearing husband who worships in spirit and truth. I want him to intercede for his family. I want him to be our protector. I want him to be obedient to you. I want to love with no strings attached. I want to give my all. I want to be a life partner. I want to know where I stand in his life, which is 2nd, while you are the 1st. These are the things I am seeking. I have gone through all I can take with him. From cheating to drugs to being in and out of jail, to gambling, to lying, to manipulation, to seem like everything is under the sun. How much does one person have to endure? So, Lord, I need you to show me where you want me to go. I can't keep doing this. I deserve the best life has to offer. I deserve to live my life and fulfill my destiny. I deserve to be happy and enjoy life instead of waiting for my husband to come home whenever he feels up to it. Lord, I don't want to cry anymore over this man. It's time for a change Lord. It's time. I love him enough to let him go, for him to be happy, and for me to be happy.

Lord, speak to me or send me an encouraging word.

Truly,
Your daughter

4

UNFORESEEN DEPARTURES: TURMOIL IN MARRIAGE

After the book event, I returned home and found that my husband had already packed his bags. My mind was filled with questions, yet the long journey had drained me. Prior to his departure, he said all he wanted was –the car he had bought me, his tools, and clothes. He said he was leaving everything else behind for us. Then he went to the kids to tell them that he was leaving as he was not content.

The following day, he left, saying he was going to stay with his mother. He took most of his possessions, and to my astonishment, he took away every piece of jewelry I owned, including my wedding ring. When I realized it, I was heartbroken. Why would he take all my jewelry?

I thought I would give him some time thinking maybe that was what he required to collect himself. *Is it possible for a forty-year-old to suffer from a midlife crisis?*

I had heard that men in their fifties often grappled with feelings of dissatisfaction, anxiety, and even depression as they navigated the transition into middle age. Perhaps my husband was experiencing this crisis earlier than most. His departure came at a particularly challenging time, coinciding with an important event in my life and exacerbating our already precarious financial situation.

> **The Guessing Game**
>
> During a separation, a narcissist might take their spouse's belongings to exert control and amplify their sense of loss and powerlessness. This act is a strategic move to destabilize the spouse and reinforce the narcissist dominance, deepening the spouse's emotional distress during an already difficult time.

With my husband gone and our finances strained due to his prolonged unemployment, I knew it would be an uphill battle to regain stability. Despite his absence, he reassured me that he remained committed to our financial well-being. He promised to contribute half of the bills, allowing us to work together towards getting our accounts back in good standing.

The week after my husband's departure, I sat down with one of my sons to go over all the bills. I started calling creditors to request a reduction on my accounts. For others, I had to set up payment plans.

> **The Guessing Game**
>
> A narcissistic husband is likely to abandon his family during financial difficulties, as he prioritizes his own comfort and status over their well-being. His departure in such times exacerbates the family's struggle, further demonstrating his disregard for their needs and reinforcing his self-centered behavior.

My son said, "Mom, you can't manage all these bills by yourself; it's too much for you."

In the face of overwhelming challenges, I leaned on my unwavering trust in God as Jehovah Jireh—the provider who never abandons His own. Despite uncertainty about our financial future and how we would fulfill our commitments, I held fast to the belief that God would never fail me. This wasn't the first time I had walked this path; throughout our 12-year marriage, I often felt burdened with the responsibility of providing for our home.

For years, I diligently managed our household finances, allocating the majority of my income to cover expenses and faithfully paying tithes from the remainder. Meanwhile, my husband's financial affairs remained largely opaque to me. While he contributed to some bills, his spending habits, such as leisure activities and indulgences, were shrouded in mystery. Despite my efforts to maintain transparency and accountability in our finances, I felt as though he exerted control over my finances while his remained elusive.

> **Narcissistic Control**
>
> The mark of the narcissist is the need to control — their environment, their partner, and every other portion of their lives while insisting on privacy and resorting to secrecy.

I began to harbor suspicions that my husband was diverting household funds without my knowledge, but I couldn't confirm it. Despite my attempts to broach the subject, he adamantly refused to open up, leaving me feeling isolated in our relationship. With each discussion about his finances, I sensed him growing more distant, deepening the rift between us.

His secretive behavior regarding his financial affairs only heightened my unease. Despite my persistent inquiries, I was met with evasiveness and obfuscation, perpetuating a sense of uncertainty and powerlessness. It felt like trying to navigate through a fog of ambiguity, with him holding all the answers close to his chest.

Determined to uncover the truth, I pressed on, but my efforts yielded no satisfactory resolution. The lack of transparency in our financial relationship left me feeling frustrated and helpless, unable to penetrate the wall of secrecy he had erected.

One day, I stumbled upon a letter from the state lottery and gaming control agency that had been delivered to our house. My husband seemed unaware that I had witnessed him tucking the letter into the pocket of his jacket in the entryway closet. Curiosity piqued, I retrieved the letter and discovered that he had won a substantial sum of money. Despite this windfall, he never disclosed anything to me about his winnings, and I didn't notice any significant influx of money into our household.

For a long time, I grappled with the sense that he was exploiting me financially, while enjoying the freedom to spend as he pleased. It felt like a one-sided dynamic, where I meticulously monitored every penny spent on bills, while he remained opaque about his financial activities. Although there were occasional gestures of generosity, they often seemed motivated by guilt rather than genuine care or consideration.

It was disheartening that whenever I bought something for my husband, he rarely appreciated it and would often find a reason to return it for a refund. One particular incident stood out: when I surprised him with gym gear to support his desire to exercise, his reaction was one of disdain. Later, he returned all the items without so much as an apology, only realizing their suitability after seeing how others were dressed at the gym. Unfortunately, this was just one example among many similar instances of ungratefulness.

Despite the challenges we faced, I firmly believed in the adage, "Where there is a will, there is a way." With God's guidance, I found a solution to our financial woes by tapping into my retirement savings. Over the years, I had frequently dipped into these savings, leaving me with little left. Nevertheless, I was able to submit a withdrawal request, hoping it would help alleviate our financial strain and cover overdue bills, including our children's tuition fees.

During the initial period of separation, my spouse continued to visit almost daily. Despite our strained relationship, I felt compelled to fulfill my wifely duties, such as preparing his meals, packing his lunches, and tending to his laundry. In my heart, I believed this was what the Lord expected of me as a wife, even in his absence. As the days passed, my prayers intensified, seeking guidance and strength from above. I frequently reached out to my husband, seeking his permission to pray for him, and he never once declined my request.

In October 2019, shortly after my husband's departure, I received a call from one of my brothers, informing me that my husband had reached out to him to reveal that he had left me. At that point, I had not disclosed his absence to anyone, as I held onto hope that he would return. Our relationship had been marked by a cycle of separations and reconciliations, and I didn't want to burden my family with yet another upheaval. Moreover, I remained steadfast in my belief in our marriage and held onto the love I had for him, hoping for his transformation.

However, as my brother shared the news circulating in our hometown about my husband's departure and his rumored return to his previous lifestyle, I couldn't help but feel a sense of disbelief and concern. Despite my reluctance to accept the rumors, there were undeniable red flags that raised alarms. I prayed fervently that he wouldn't revert to the life from which God had rescued him numerous times before. The thought that he may have left to return to the streets weighed heavily on my heart, leaving me with unanswered questions and aching uncertainty.

Despite longing for my husband's return, I felt a tremendous weight lifted from my being, bringing with it a sense of peace. I noticed that things around the house started to improve. My countenance changed as I experienced a newfound sense of energy and joy. The boys and I were soon accustomed to our new order. Our home was always kept neat. I prayed for our abode to be protected from any evil. I could feel a sense of serenity in the air. My husband saw the alterations and asked how the house could be running more smoothly without him. I was unsure of what he was searching for, but I knew that God had given me newfound strength, self-assurance, and fearlessness.

Amid the hardship I was going through, I learned to express myself more, using my talents and gifts. I had a longing to keep control of my situation rather than letting it control my state of mind. Subsequently, I worked more with the ministry God assigned me to — Women of Destiny Empowerment Ministry. I met with other women at my local library for one hour on Thursday nights to talk about female empowerment. A lot of the ladies in the group were like me; we had something in common, going through a separation or divorce.

To top it off, I officially opened my coaching company — Designed for Greatness, Finding Your Purpose and quickly signed two clients. In spite of the problems I faced in my marriage, God opened opportunities for me to discuss my book on various platforms and advertise my business to local colleges and universities to generate additional streams of income.

Speaking of colleges, one of our sons, who was away in college, reached out to me and informed me of his unbearable agony due to a recent knee operation. His desperate call for help necessitated my urgent attention, so I contacted my husband to let him know about our son's condition and the need to go to the university to attend to our son. At first, my husband did not want to go, offering me his car, and suggesting I take one of our kids along with me. I firmly responded that no matter what we were going through, our child required both his parents, and he was coming along.

He felt he had to evaluate the seriousness of the issue, so he phoned our son to ask about his distress. I guess he called to ensure I was telling the truth, but why would I lie about such a thing? In the end, he agreed to come with me on the drive for three hours.

On our drive to visit our son, my husband telephoned his mother to inform her that he was travelling with me to our son; I found it quite odd. However, I didn't have time to think about it. Can I say something unusual occurred to me on that drive? It wasn't bizarre; it was extraordinary. I prayed in my heavenly language the entire time. For whatever reason, I couldn't stop. The Holy Spirit overwhelmed me. My husband didn't murmur a word. Each time I tried to stop, I couldn't.

When we arrived at my son's dormitory, we took him directly to the emergency room where a doctor examined him. It appeared from the x-ray that he had reinjured his knee. He was discharged with instructions to begin therapy promptly. We left the emergency room and helped our son get situation back to his dorm before returning home.

The journey back home felt longer than the one that led us away. About halfway through, I summoned the courage to initiate a conversation with my spouse, hoping to understand the reasons behind his sudden departure. Until that moment, we hadn't broached the subject. He began by expressing his belief that I no longer loved him, a notion that puzzled me as it didn't align with anything I had conveyed. I hadn't uttered words of disdain or a desire to end our relationship.

When I questioned him about the basis for his assumption, he cited our past struggles and implied that it was time for us to part ways. I inquired if there was someone else involved, which he adamantly denied. For the next hour, I pleaded with him to reconsider, emphasizing the impact his decision would have on our two children, one of whom was a high school senior and the other in their last year of middle school. Additionally, I highlighted his failure to communicate any dissatisfaction or desire to separate prior to his departure, underscoring the unfairness of making such a unilateral decision without involving me in the discussion.

I felt he had deceived me.

We hadn't reached a mutual agreement to end our marriage, and I struggled to comprehend how my husband could abruptly pack his belongings and leave his family without discussing it with me first. His actions appeared self-centered, focused solely on his own desires while disregarding the impact on our children. Despite my pleas, he refused to consider counseling, citing previous unsuccessful attempts.

Our history with counseling was checkered. The first time, we sought help from our church pastor and his wife. During the sessions, I voiced concerns about my husband's constant marijuana use and described our marriage as feeling more like a business arrangement. In response, my husband criticized my appearance and admitted to emotional connections with other women, including one from his workplace. Despite the pastor's guidance to prioritize our marriage and cease drug use, my husband left the session in anger, feeling ganged up on.

> **Narcissistic Deception**
>
> Selfishness and deception are the armor the narcissist wears to keep people at bay. Though they start romantic relationships by love bombing, pouring out their love, once the relationship is secure, they retreat into themselves.

Our second attempt at counseling came after my husband returned from a work trip, fearful of losing me due to his interaction with another woman and concerns about a sexually transmitted disease. We attended three sessions with a certified marriage therapist, during which my husband appeared to make efforts to improve. However, his commitment waned after a few months, and he reverted to his old habits. Despite these setbacks, I remained hopeful that counseling could help salvage our marriage.

As we drove home from our son's university, I made a heartfelt plea for my husband to consider moving into our basement, emphasizing the importance of his presence for our children. However, his response remained resolute - a firm "no." It was evident that my words had little effect on him; his decision seemed firmly fixed in his mind.

Seeking answers, I questioned him about why he had taken my wedding ring. In response, he reached into the car's middle console and retrieved the ring, handing it back to me. With a mix of emotions, I accepted the ring and gently placed it back on my finger.

We talked more about the reason he left. He stated that he wasn't content. He couldn't tell me why and directed everything at me. He claimed I wasn't pleased. *How can he tell me how I feel?* I wanted him to be bold enough to tell me the truth so I could either get closure or battle for our marriage. I said I wouldn't beg or fight for something he didn't want or that no longer served him.

A preacher once said that people don't abandon people they love; they abandon people they were using. And when you're no longer of any use, they move on. He made it clear that he no longer wanted the marriage.

With a heavy heart, I removed my wedding ring, unable to bear the weight of its symbolism amidst the shattered promises and unfulfilled vows. Handing it back to him, I felt a sense of finality wash over me. As I sobbed, I knew that there was nothing left for me to do or say; his decision was made.

Arriving back home in the early hours of the morning, my husband asked if he could stay for a few hours, and I reluctantly agreed. Retreating to my room, I was startled by a knock on the door. Welcoming him in, I took a seat on the bed as he settled into a chair, ready to listen.

As he spoke, acknowledging his failure to communicate and expressing his mistaken belief that the separation was my desire, I listened intently, my heart heavy with the weight of our misunderstandings and the pain of our broken vows.

These were his words:

"Cheryl, I want you to listen to me. You say I never talk or communicate with you. Please listen to me. I want you to know that I love you and will always love you. I want you to take care of yourself. I always want to be your friend. You can call and talk to me at any time about anything. The only thing that is off-limits is I don't want to hear about you and another man or having another man. When that time comes, I want you to get someone who is better than me. Someone who will take you to all the places you wanted to go that I never took you to. I want you to get a man who will treat you like a queen, open and close your door. Someone who will be there for you no matter what. Someone who will protect you like you want and need to be protected. Find someone who will not break their promises to you. I want you to find happiness. I want you to learn what makes you happy. Take the time to learn about yourself. I see you are losing weight; keep going, and don't stop. I want you to get your perfumes. Purchase your clothes. Do all the things that will make you happy. I want you to keep advancing in your career. You have come a long way. Please keep going until you get that supervisory position. Keep climbing to GS-14, then GS-15 position. I know you will be successful. I want to let you know that I

love you and want you to be happy. I can't be the person you want me to be."

As he concluded his heartfelt speech, tears streamed down both our faces, marking the end of our journey together. His words, his "Goodbye Love" speech, echoed in my mind, leaving me shattered and bewildered. Despite his tears, I struggled to comprehend what had led him to this decision. His reasons seemed to point away from himself, focusing instead on perceived shortcomings within me.

His departure, though expected, left me reeling with confusion and pain. I had sought closure, but now I found myself grappling with more questions than answers. The wounds of incomprehension and unworthiness pierced deep within me, leaving me feeling lost and betrayed.

Just when I thought the turmoil couldn't deepen further, the arrival of divorce papers from the sheriff's office shattered any semblance of understanding. Sitting on the front porch, I stared at the paperwork in disbelief, grappling with the reality that he had initiated divorce proceedings while we were still under the same roof. The suddenness of it all left me questioning his motives and the haste with which he sought to end our marriage.

After 12 years of marriage, I sat holding documents to bring an end to our marriage due to differences that were beyond repair. I couldn't believe what was happening. There was no way to explain the feelings that I was feeling. I was paralyzed, completely shocked by the fact that he was planning the divorce without me even knowing it.

The following day I was unable to go to work with my heart shattered into a million pieces. The person I loved didn't feel the same way toward me anymore. How could he take such drastic measures? How can someone give their all and still be treated like the villain? What did I do wrong other than loving him? I gave him more than my love; I gave him my everything, and it was still not enough. Was I perfect? No, no one is. But was I a bad person? No.

He conveyed to me that he believed I excelled in only three areas:

Praying, Playing, and Paying. It was an observation I couldn't deny. He often relied on my prayers for our family and others in need, recognizing the calling of intercession in my life. We frequently visited hospitals together so I could offer prayers for the sick, a duty he respected and supported.

When it came to financial matters, he acknowledged my dedication to ensuring bills were paid, even at my own expense. I often covered the shortfall when he failed to contribute, resulting in damaged credit and financial strain. This aspect of our relationship left me feeling financially exploited.

In terms of playfulness, I made efforts to bring joy into our lives through humor and light-hearted moments. However, I couldn't shake the feeling that I fell short in loving him the way he desired and needed. Despite this, my love for him was unwavering and unconditional, mirroring the love I felt from God.

The situation caught me off guard. As I reviewed the court document outlining a thirty-day response period, I realized I needed legal assistance. The prospect of affording a lawyer seemed daunting, considering my recent withdrawals from my retirement savings to cover expenses. I reached out to a lawyer friend from my church, explaining my predicament and seeking advice. She suggested attending a law clinic hosted by our church the following Saturday, where I could meet with a family law attorney and discuss my options.

I attended the law clinic as recommended by my friend, where I met the colleague she had mentioned. I presented the legal papers I had received, and she scheduled an appointment for me at her office the following Monday. Ahead of the meeting, she sent me a list of required documents, including financial statements, retirement records, and a comprehensive inventory of all my bills. The task felt overwhelming, stirring up considerable anxiety within me.

Arriving at the lawyer's office on the designated Monday, we discussed her fees and charges. I expressed uncertainty about my ability to afford her services. However, she assured me that, as a member of ASBC, I would receive a discount and could initiate a payment plan beginning the next year. To kickstart the paperwork for an absolute divorce, I needed to provide an initial payment of $1100.00.

One of her initial inquiries was regarding the duration of our separation. I explained that my husband had left almost a month prior. She questioned the rationale behind his request for an absolute divorce when we hadn't been separated for the required duration. In the state we resided, she clarified, a full divorce based on voluntary separation could only be obtained after both parties had lived apart in separate residences without sexual interaction for twelve months. It seemed my husband may have been misinformed about the necessary documents and procedures.

The lawyer inquired whether I wished to battle for my marriage. I said that it was pointless to contest since my husband had already made up his mind to end the union. She then asked if I believed he had a child from an extramarital affair. I honestly told her that I was unaware of such a thing, though I had asked him a few times if he had any other children, to which he would always say no. I was uncertain whether he was being honest or not.

My husband seemed to have a clandestine life. It was possible that he had an entire family somewhere. He was secretive and a master of deceit. I had encountered numerous lies from him during our marriage. However, I had no solid evidence — only hearsay, which would not be permissible in a court of law. Still, I confessed that there were rumors of him fathering another woman's baby. This speculation had been circulating for quite some time. I did not know if it was valid since he never acknowledged it, nor did anyone talk to me about having another child.

The lawyer continued to ask some difficult questions. For most of them, I had an answer. Others... well... I did not. This was the commencement of a prolonged journey which I was not pleased about. But I had no other option. My husband had left me with no choice but to protect myself and our children.

5

TRUSTING IN DREAMS: THE PATH TO FORGIVENESS

Navigating through a legal separation was an arduous journey that weighed heavily on me. My husband and I established a temporary arrangement for the minor children still at home. Initially, he agreed to have them on weekends, which seemed to work smoothly at first. However, as time went on, he consistently found reasons to cancel or fail to show up. Watching the disappointment on our children's faces as they waited for him filled me with sorrow.

On one occasion, he had planned an eagerly anticipated fishing trip for the kids and some friends from his former workplace. However, on the morning of the trip, he called to cancel, leaving our boys crestfallen. Shortly after, he asked if I could contribute financially to cover the costs of the trip, which amounted to $125 per child. Despite my reluctance, I couldn't bear to see the kids let down, so I drove an hour to provide him with the money.

Unfortunately, this act of generosity seemed to set a precedent. He began to view me as his personal ATM, regularly requesting money despite not upholding his end of the agreement to split the bills equally. Meanwhile, I was left shouldering the responsibility of keeping our household afloat while he resided rent-free with his mother. Despite my empathy for his situation, I continued to transfer money into his account as requested.

More than ever, I felt a deep calling in my heart to continuously pray for my husband. Toward the end of October, I was led to go on a fast for him. I petitioned God for his protection. I sensed something was wrong with him, but I didn't know what that could be. Word was still circulating that he was "in the streets," participating in unlawful activities. One day, when our son had his father's car, he found marijuana in the vehicle. My son took a photo and sent it to me. I was so livid with my husband. I texted him with the snapshot to tell him not to put our son's life and freedom in danger. While I couldn't stop him from smoking or doing whatever he was doing, the kids were my responsibility, and it was my obligation to look out for their safety and well-being.

Discovering that my husband had allowed our son to drive his pickup truck with expired tags for over thirty minutes left me furious and deeply concerned for our son's safety. It was incomprehensible to me how he could endanger our child in such a reckless manner. What baffled me even more was the fact that he would never have taken the same risk himself but had no qualms about subjecting our son to it. I immediately expressed my outrage to him through text and email, emphasizing the gravity of his actions.

Simultaneously, my attorney diligently worked on our divorce case, swiftly responding to my husband's filings with relevant paperwork submitted to the courts. When my husband realized that I had legal representation despite our precarious financial situation, he was visibly agitated. He reached out to a relative to inquire about how I managed to afford a lawyer and vowed not to be defeated without a fight.

A few days later, my husband returned to our home appearing dejected, asserting that neither of us could afford legal representation. He sought to negotiate directly with me, expressing his intention to hire a lawyer and implying that he could not afford one. However, I remained resolute in my decision to proceed with legal counsel, advising him to seek legal assistance through the courts. Despite his dissatisfaction with my response, I stood firm, recognizing that his actions had repeatedly demonstrated his lack of consideration for my well-being and best interests.

The more I prayed for my husband, the more I would have these intense dreams about him. There was one dream on October 31st that had me shaken to the core.

> *In my dream, I stumbled upon my recently deceased uncle, a mortician, standing at a distance in a black and white suit at Dunkin Donuts while I was ordering some coffee. I felt petrified and immediately told my husband that we had to leave that place immediately. As I exited the building, I was alone.*
>
> *On my walk from the coffee shop, I ran into my departed cousin who was on her new assignment in the heavens. I asked her about her job, and she revealed that she was a guardian and that her duties were still unclear. We then came to a park where the ground was soaked from the recent rain and the trees had orange and brown foliage, signifying that it was autumn. I chose to go a different way since the ground was still damp. We carried on our conversation, and I asked how she pays her bills in heaven. She said that she just enters the details of her account, like one would with an electric bill, and then the amount is deducted. I inquired if I, too, had this power here on earth, to which she looked at me with a puzzled face. With that, I awoke from the dream.*

Part II

In this dream, I was on a university campus, which gave me a feeling of a local college. I was accompanied by my friend, Gabrielle. We went to the student center where many learners were conversing and displaying their creations. I paused at a table and interacted with one of the students. Soon after, we were ready to leave. We ran into an old high school PE instructor who talked to us for a while. After the talk, we sprinted out of the building and towards a car, which was my husband's Old Mustang Cobra. Peculiarly, there was a lot of chatter about the car and how the police had been notified because there were narcotics in the car. I was perplexed as to what was happening. Then I awakened.

My dreams grew increasingly vivid, serving as a conduit for divine communication. Throughout my life, I had been a dreamer, and I recognized this as one of the ways in which God chose to speak to me. Often prophetic in nature, my dreams held hidden messages, prompting me to pray earnestly and meticulously record each one. While some dreams came with immediate interpretations from God, others required patience as I awaited their unfolding.

God frequently used my dreams as warnings, especially concerning my husband. Despite sharing these dreams with him, he often dismissed them. Yet, this year alone, I experienced numerous dreams involving him, his friends, and other relatives. As I fervently interceded for him, these dreams became more frequent, prompting me to carefully note their details and seek divine guidance for their meanings. Though many of these dreams disrupted my sleep, I recognized them as messages from God and committed to fervent prayer, trusting in His wisdom and guidance.

On the November 5th, I had another dream, and the Lord graciously provided me with the interpretation:

As I sat in the rear seat of a car, one of my husband's relatives was in the front pushing her seat onto me, leaving me confounded as to why she would do such a thing. When we got out of the car, we were in my parents' backyard. I was still seated behind her, and she was attempting to take my place again by shifting her chair into mine. I got up, and it seemed like a family gathering was taking place at my parents' house. I remembered seeing a lot of fish there. I was abruptly awakened from the dream.

This is the interpretation of the dream God gave me:

"My daughter, I am showing you where the enemy is lurking. He will use whomever he pleases to kill, steal, and destroy. Unfortunately, many people are being used by the enemy and don't realize it. But I want you to be aware of the plots and schemes of the enemy. The enemy will have it where they are so envious sometimes, they will go to extreme measures. I want you to be alert and pray as you did this morning. Things are turning around, says the spirit of the living God. The devil may have thought he had you, but he will be sad to know you are about to soar like never before. Eyes have not seen nor ears heard what the everlasting God has for you. Just know that his plots, schemes, and devices will not work. You will come out victorious like never before. Keep the faith. Keep trusting in me. Keep praying and fasting (fast as the Holy Spirit leads you). There is so much in store for you, great things! The Lord says you should not take your eyes off him. Keep moving with grace and dignity. You are always on the Father's mind and in his heart. Your breakthrough is here, says the Lord. Doors are opening one behind the other. Keep your focus and trust in me."

God was exerting His influence in my life in numerous ways. Various opportunities were presented to me to promote my book on numerous platforms. I had a couple of radio interviews scheduled on live broadcasts in different states. The initial one was local. I implored God concerning what He wanted me to communicate with the listeners. I perceived God urging me to talk about forgiveness. "I want you to forgive your husband," I heard a voice say. Was I discernibly hearing God? Why would He want me to offer forgiveness when my husband was the one who left his family? I was constantly asking for forgiveness, being the bigger person in every situation. I did this to maintain harmony. But now, God desired me to proclaim to millions of listeners my forgiveness. I didn't understand, yet I God gave my "Yes!"

At my initial interview, I sat there with my jotted down ideas, and bided my time as the host had another guest. When the host got to me, it was long before all the preliminary questions which had been sent to me earlier had been asked and answered. But then, the host started talking about "Forgiveness." I remember saying that I had to forgive myself, as self-forgiveness is derived from understanding God's mercy.

The Bible makes it clear that all people have committed sin against God (**Romans 3:23**) and that all our wrongdoings are against Him (**Psalm 51:4; Genesis 39:9**). Therefore, what we require is God's grace, which is obtainable to us through Jesus Christ. Those who have faith in Jesus will be completely pardoned of their sins. They are thought of as righteous before God, eternally justified (**Romans 5:1–11; Ephesians 1:13–14; 2:1–10**). Though we still contend with sin, God stays faithful to cleanse us when we admit our mistakes to Him and renew our relationship with Him (**1 John 1:9; 2:1–2**). The sacrifice of Jesus was ample to cover any of our sins. Thus, forgiving yourself essentially has to do with accepting God's forgiveness.

In addition, I expressed how forgiving oneself can be especially arduous when our misbehavior has had an adverse effect on someone else. It is essential to seek absolution from those we have wronged and to reconcile where possible. Again, God is the one who enables this unification. Living in disgrace will not set right a shattered relationship or take away the hurt we have inflicted. But the veracity of the gospel can. At this point, on live radio, I humbly asked for my husband's forgiveness. I asked him to forgive me for not being the wife he wanted me to be, for not living up to his desires, and for not loving him the way he longed to be loved. As I was speaking, my voice quivered. I wanted to weep, but I had to maintain my composure. As I ended the interview, I felt a sense of triumph. I did what God directed me to do. The remainder was up to him.

In the days following the radio interviews, my husband made an unexpected visit to our house. I granted him permission to take a shower, and as he prepared to enter the bathroom, a wave of emotion overcame me, leading me to apologize for any wrongs I may have committed and express my forgiveness towards him. Though he had not sought it, I felt compelled to assure him of my forgiveness.

Then, driven by a sudden surge of emotion, I began to pray fervently, pouring out my heart to the Lord on behalf of my husband. Tears flowed freely as I uttered the words the Holy Spirit placed on my heart. His expression betrayed a sense of bewilderment as my prayers unfolded, and though I could not fully comprehend the depth of my emotions, I felt compelled to convey a message from God, warning him to veer away from the path leading to his downfall. Our prayer concluded with a heartfelt embrace, and he reciprocated, expressing his own forgiveness before leaving our home after completing his shower.

That night, memories of the joyful moments we shared over the twelve years of our marriage flooded my thoughts. In my journal, I chronicled each cherished memory, from his infectious smile and laughter to the tender acts of care, like his attempts to style my hair or trim my nails. Despite the challenges we faced, his kindness and generosity of spirit never wavered, and I held deep admiration for him. The simple gestures, like hearing him call my name or seeing him open and close doors for me, filled me with warmth and nostalgia.

Amidst the longing for happier times, memories of our shared experiences brought bittersweet solace. I recalled the humorous mishap in the shower, where we nearly stumbled and fell, laughing together in the process. Our early courtship was marked by excitement and passion, evident in our impromptu expressions of love during trips to various cities. Even in sickness, he remained a pillar of support, caring for me with tenderness and compassion, despite his own ailments.

I persisted with my solemn prayers for my spouse, and I felt the Lord bestowing me with these words with respect to my husband:

(Love Letters to God, November 11, 2019).

November 11, 2019

Allow the Holy Spirit to lead & guide you.

This is a new DAY, A NEW season for you. Just as the leaves change to denote fall — it is your transitional season. It will bring about your HARVEST (Fall = HARVEST = GATHERING) Transition into the new.

** I am going to put him away for a while to work on him. During this time you will blossom into that flower I have called you into being. Don't worry about him; he will be safe & from danger, b/ I need to get the filimy in his life & this situation. He want be gone for long. But, while he's there I will work on him from the inside/out. I will take care of you & your house. There will not be lack; b/ abundance. I have to do this says the Lord. It

"Those who exalt themselves will be humbled, and those who humble themselves will be exalted."

November 11, 2019

is my way of protecting him — from himself. You continue to pray as I lead. Just know that I the Lord am working all things out for my good.

It's not going to be long from now says the Lord when this shall occur. Yes, you are hearing correctly. I have warned (showed) you in your dream; now I am speaking to you. No one can blame you for his actions since he left you. I want you to know, he will be better.

I, the Lord want you to keep doing the things I have placed on you to do. I will bless all areas of your life. Claim Nehemiah 2 over your life. I am sending you forth to build for me. Where I send, favor will be w/ you. You will have all the Resources you need. Your children will be fine; I will provide for him

"Do not be afraid, for I have ransomed you. I have called you by name; you are Mine. When you go through deep waters, I will be with you."

Isa. 43:1-2

November 11, 2019

I will bless you w/ everything you need & desire says the Lord. I will strengthen you more & more each day. I will give you peace beyond your understanding. It's time says the Lord for you to Reap the ~~Harvest~~; Eph 3:20, Gal 6:9

Let us not become weary in doing good for at the proper time we will reap a harvest if we do not give up.

My Grace, y the burdens you carry is not yours, b/ everyone else. It's time for you to enjoy life. To do the things that brings fulfillment to you. I want (it is my desire) to see you happy; not lacking no good thing, but perfect in all things (ways) I know the things you've gone through; I was with you. I know the hurt & pain you felt. I felt

Nov 11, 2019

it as well. The TURNAROUND is now! You will almost forget the years past for where I am leading you is different. You will reap differently. The blessings are yours says the Lord! Blessed is the child who endures divers temptations; who endures the hardships of life. Blessed is he who does not fail or give in (give up). Blessed is he who perseveres in the midst of everything.

But woe to the ones who tries to come against my anointed one in these days. Woe to the ones who try to curse my chosen vessels, they will be put to shame and exposed for their wickedness says the Lord.

Claim Nehemiah 2 daughter, it is your portion this day moving forward.

My journal turned out to be my, "Love Letters to God", which contained numerous dreams I had in the prior months. I interpreted them as a sign of a changeover from the old to the new. I was not sure of the full implications of what the Lord was showing me. He had previously implied that my dreams had a prophetic nature, and that they would come to fruition at His appointed time.

Dream April 19, 2019, Morning around 8-9 am

> *I was seated in the kitchen when one of my sons' and his father appeared in front of me. Astonishingly, I watched as my son morphed into his dad before my eyes and I promptly fainted. Immediately, I sensed the presence of God as a voice came to my aid. I could feel Him fanning me, waiting for me to return to consciousness. Subsequently, a vision of a huge blazing fire was unveiled to me. A voice from the flames declared that I had entered a new season with fresh beginnings. The Lord announced that I would no longer remain in my current state but rather, He was transforming my life. Out with the old and in with the new; He promised to turn everything around for my benefit.*

October 20, 2019, Dream

> *I had a dream in the morning in which I was leaving a place of familiarity and setting out for an unfamiliar area. I was on a train in a big city; I believed it was New York since my cousin Lisa was sitting behind me, and she resides there. My youngest son and I were both on the train. My husband was there, sitting behind us on the other side. He got up and gave me a $10.00 ticket; then, it decreased to $8.00. I needed it to reach my destination. He left the train, but before he did, I asked him, "Where am I going?" He answered, "She would*

show you how to get to where you need to be," referring to my cousin. *I felt scared. I looked to make sure my son was in sight since I didn't want to lose him. Other passengers were on the train, but I was unaware of them. I continued this train ride, and I was awakened from the dream.*

6

TURMOIL AND TRIALS: THE UNRAVELING OF TRUTH

One morning in November, my husband dropped off his car for our son to drive. With our son now having a part-time job after school, we needed an additional vehicle for his transportation. As I processed this arrangement, I noticed a parking pass for Regatta Bay Apartments inside my husband's car. This revelation puzzled me; he was supposed to be staying with his mother, but it seemed there was more to the story. I couldn't recall anyone we knew residing there. My son had already taken a photo of the pass and sent it to me.

Despite the practical need for another vehicle, I couldn't shake off the unease about my son driving his dad's car. I worried about the lifestyle my husband might be leading or the activities he might be involved in. Amidst these concerns, I continued to lean on prayer, faithfully anointing my van daily and seeking God's protection for safe travels. I entrusted my journey to His care, praying for the guidance and protection of His ministering angels on the highways and byways.

On November 22ⁿᵈ, I called into Prophetess Kimberly Moses' afternoon prayer call. She opened the lines to receive prayer requests. I asked for prayer (specifically for a vehicle), and the woman of God spoke the following words:

"You are about to receive a mind-blowing miracle.

-Thank you for the new car; I don't know how you're going to do it; I see her signing the papers, signing the checks, getting the car; driving off the lot.

-Thank you for this move; the right car-reliable; not overpriced.

-The Lord is going to bless you with a financial increase. There is a promotion God wants to bring to you with employment. Shifting more pay per hour.

-God is going to be working with you with your credit to clear up some debts; he is going to give you strategies to invest and save.

-People will give a season of favor. Unusual favor for money.

-God loves you so much-doesn't want you to be in lack or confused.

Outside of this situation, some things happened that left you confused-in relationships that caused you to be confused. God doesn't want you to be confused. He's saying, daughter, when I showed you the person's heart; don't doubt what I have shown you. When I show you their motives, don't doubt them and don't go back. Please don't go back to the things I am moving from you, and don't question me b/c I have your best interest at heart.

-There are some gifts inside of you, and you're frustrated with those gifts in your life, and you're saying, "I don't fit in here... no one is asking me to do something. Wait and be patient. As you wait and focus on Jesus, God will put those gifts in demand, and he will pull out gifts inside of you -you didn't know you possessed.

-I see you singing. God will put melodies in your heart for you to sing prophetically. As you sing, there will be fire, the glory, and the presence of God will be so strong people will begin to shake and tremble.

-I thank God there will be no more confusion, and her faith is going to another level.

-I give you praise for the supernatural funds.

The Lord wants you to go deeper into worship times 4. Remind God of the words from today.

-God says he has a car for you, and I see you driving off the lot. I saw you signing the paperwork and the keys before me. God is going to bless you to get in a car.

-God will do something supernatural in your credit; God says go worship; as you worship, there will be a supernatural portal to open up over your life.

-The Lord says he is assigning you an angel of finance. To your assignment, your purchase, your destiny, to underwrite some of the costs. God is sending an angel of finance as a sign *that I am with you; that I come to prosper you; a sign to heal you emotionally; even to restore things in your family; even in relationships. In the name of Jesus.*

Have a worshiping heart! I see an angel of finance. God has you."

A few days after that prayer call, I felt the Lord's assurance in my spirit. He told me to have faith and assured me that I would not be left alone. On that day, I decided to trust God's word and the blessing of that woman of God. Even though I had an unfavorable credit score, I chose to apply for a pre-owned car while on my lunch break at work. A few moments later, I got a call from the sales representative to enquire about the type of car I desired. I didn't pay much heed to it as all I wanted was something more dependable than my current vehicle.

After my workday ended, I visited the dealership, where they informed me that, based on my credit, I was eligible for a new vehicle. The sales representative consulted with the loan officer and returned to ask about my preferences. I knew I needed a vehicle with a third-row seat to comfortably accommodate our family of five. They presented two options: a white Kia Sorento and a gray one. Opting for the gray model, I waited nearly forty-five minutes before being called to the back to complete the paperwork.

During this time, the loan officer apologized for the delay, explaining that she had to contact the bank due to an error in my loan. Surprisingly, the bank confirmed that the interest rate provided was accurate, which puzzled me. According to my credit score, the interest rate should have been much higher, possibly exceeding 28%. Despite the confusion, I felt overwhelming gratitude at that moment. It seemed that the Lord had intervened, just as the prophet had foretold. The prophet had spoken of a miraculous change in my credit and the provision of a financial angel to finance the vehicle. Overwhelmed with emotion, I could only weep.

Even the loan officer recognized the divine intervention, remarking that she had never witnessed anything like it in her more than twenty years of experience in the car industry.

Returning home that evening, I couldn't help but celebrate God for His provision. I invited the kids to admire our new car as I pulled into the garage. Their excitement matched my own, and we were all filled with joy. Acquiring the car just before the Thanksgiving holiday felt like a blessing.

With the car ready, I decided we should take a trip to South Carolina to be with family. I felt a strong desire to surround ourselves with loved ones during the holiday. When my other two boys arrived, I informed them of our plans. However, my husband questioned our itinerary, expressing his wish to spend time with the kids before they returned to school. I assured him that we would be back by Saturday to ensure he could enjoy quality time with them.

The mini trip to be with family proved to be exactly what we needed. Surrounded by laughter and good food, we relished the time spent together. However, during our visit, I couldn't help but overhear rumors circulating about my husband. There were whispers suggesting that he had left me because he was tired of supporting me, insinuating that I didn't work or contribute financially. While I chose not to confront these baseless rumors, I couldn't ignore them entirely. Additionally, there were talks about his recent trips to Miami, New York, and South Carolina, with some speculating that he was heavily involved in drug use. Unsure of the truth behind these rumors, I couldn't help but wonder about his actions in his newfound single life.

Our trip came to an end as we returned home as promised on Saturday after Thanksgiving. The children phoned their dad to tell him they were back and desired to see him. He said one of his close relatives was in town and that he would see them later. He never showed up that day. He came the following morning to take one of our sons back to college.

On that Monday evening following Thanksgiving, my husband showed up at the house to retrieve his car. He said he'd return later. After a few hours, he reappeared with a new cell phone for our youngest son, and I was about to say something, but the Holy Spirit silenced me. I was sitting on the couch, with our son beside me. When my husband prepared to leave, our son immediately stood up and embraced him, profusely thanking him for the phone. My husband then turned to me to say that I need not be concerned about him disturbing me any longer. I didn't mumble a word as he walked out the door.

> *In the early morning hours of the next day, I dreamt I was in an unknown place. There were people with me (a few of my children). I recalled seeing two close relatives of my husband. For some odd reason, one of them was trying to give me a prescription bottle of pills. She said I needed to take it and said she got it from the children's doctor. I told her it was not my doctor and how /why would a doctor give her medicine for me; I was not sick. I recalled seeing the pill bottle but could not identify the name. She was adamant about me taking these pills.*
>
> *The dream shifted to me being inside my house. I was now looking out the window as I saw all these people (my neighbors) walking down the sidewalk to a meeting about the increasing property value. I recalled them saying how a new developer had come in to revitalize the area, thus causing our properties to soar in value.*
>
> *That day, I prayed to God these are the words he gave me: --Daughter, everything is within your reach. Ask - you shall receive. Let your joy be known. Enter my gates with Thanksgiving and into my courts with praise. Praise me, my daughter, for your promises are near thee. Daughter, know that no weapon formed against you shall prosper. You who take delight in me shall get the desires of their heart. I,*

the Lord, will never leave nor forsake you, says the Lord. I will always be here with you. This is your HARVEST time, says the Lord. I have gathered you from all the places I have scattered you, and now that I have called you back to your rightful place and position, it is time to reap a harvest. Doors will open one behind the other. Checks are coming in the mail, one after the other. The blessings will overtake thee.

I don't want you to worry or be consumed with your husband; let me take care of him. You have tried to fix him multiple times; now, allow me, your heavenly Father, to do the job. His days are numbered with his current lifestyle, says the Lord. I can no longer stand and see him self-destruct. I will guard the kids' hearts. You continue to press on and press through. There is greater waiting for you on the other side of this. No longer will you be bound in chains and your mouth cut off. No, the time has arrived for you to be ushered into the wonderful and miraculous things of the Lord. Many will apologize to you for how they have treated you. Continue to pray, intercede, and watch me move. Don't worry about the finances because I've got you. The blessings of the Lord add no sorrow.

PART II

THE FAMILY FACADE—NAVIGATING THE WEBS OF BETRAYAL WOVEN BY NARCISSISTIC ABUSE

Narcissistic abuse extends far beyond the actions of the perpetrator, intricately weaving a web of manipulation that ensnares everyone within the victim's sphere. Narcissists are adept at charming and deceiving those around them, maintaining a facade of virtue while simultaneously fabricating falsehoods about their victims. This skillful manipulation creates a misleading narrative that garners sympathy and support from family, friends, and colleagues, painting themselves as the wronged party. By distorting reality, they turn others against the true victim, isolating their target and consolidating their control. This deliberate distortion not only deflects attention from their own abusive behavior but also deepens the victim's emotional and psychological suffering, resulting in a complex maze of fractured relationships and distorted truths that complicate the victim's journey toward recovery and justice.

Even after a narcissist's death, the insidious effects of their manipulation can persist through the actions of their family members. Driven by a desire to protect the deceased's tarnished legacy, these individuals may continue to perpetuate harmful behaviors, spreading malicious gossip and fabricating stories to discredit the true victims and obscure the nature of the deceased's abuse. This ongoing deceit is fueled by a need to preserve the narcissist's image and avoid confronting uncomfortable truths. By manipulating public perception and perpetuating lies, the family members shield the deceased from scrutiny while further victimizing those who suffered under the narcissist's influence. This additional layer of deceit impedes genuine healing and adds significant complexity to the victims' struggle for justice and recognition, making the path to recovery even more arduous.

In the upcoming chapters, you will delve into the multifaceted nature of narcissistic abuse, with a focus on the betrayal and manipulation perpetuated by the narcissist's family towards the true victim. This section will explore how the abuse extends beyond the narcissist's direct actions to include various forms of harm inflicted by their family members, including emotional, social, financial, and mental abuse, as well as identity theft. You will gain insight into how family members exacerbate the victim's suffering by undermining their identity and resources.

Part II contains potentially triggering content related to these abuses, including:

- **Emotional Betrayal**: Examples of how the narcissist's family members further undermine the victim's emotional stability through deceit, manipulation, or neglect.
- **Social Isolation**: How family members contribute to the victim's social alienation by cutting them off from support networks or spreading harmful misinformation.
- **Financial Exploitation**: Instances where the victim's financial resources are controlled, depleted, or misused by the narcissist and their family.
- **Mental Manipulation**: Psychological tactics used by the family to destabilize the victim's mental health and sense of reality.
- **Identity Theft**: Cases where family members facilitate or engage in the theft and misuse of the victim's personal identity, complicating their recovery and well-being.

THE FRACTURED TRUTH: A WEB OF DECEPTION AND GRIEF

December 4th, 2019 will forever remain etched in my memory as the day I received the devastating news of my husband's passing. The shock was so profound that I found myself unable to form coherent words, my screams echoing in the silence of the night. My son, alerted by the commotion, rushed to my side as I handed him the phone before collapsing under the weight of grief. In that moment, the world seemed to stop, and I was engulfed by a whirlwind of emotions too overwhelming to comprehend.

In the aftermath of the heartbreaking news, I struggled to come to terms with the reality of my husband's death. Desperate for confirmation, I reached out to the authorities, seeking any information they could provide about the circumstances surrounding his passing. Speaking to the investigator assigned to the case, I sought answers, my heart heavy with dread. Learning that a notification of his death had been attempted at our home, only to go unanswered, intensified the surreal nature of the situation. It was a moment of agonizing disbelief, as I grappled with the incomprehensible loss of my husband.

It was reported that on December 3, 2019, emergency units responded to a report of an unresponsive male in his vehicle. The details shared by the investigator shed some light on the possible cause of my husband's untimely demise, suggesting the likelihood of a stroke or heart attack. As I sought clarification and closure, the investigator's responses provided some measure of reassurance amidst the overwhelming grief.

With the investigation concluded and no signs of foul play detected, I was notified that I could retrieve his belongings from the station. It was a bittersweet task, tinged with the poignant reminder of his absence. Yet, the officer's assurance that his passing bore no suspicious undertones offered a glimmer of solace amid the darkness of mourning. As I prepared to collect his belongings, I knew that his memory would forever remain cherished in my heart.

After I disconnected the phone from the investigator, I reached out to some of my family members. The hardest part was reaching out to my sons at college. I contacted their universities and spoke with grief counselors at both schools, sharing the heartbreaking news of their father's death. I asked for someone to be with them when I made the call, and each college responded by sending a counselor to support the boys during that difficult moment. They even helped arrange for one of my sons to return home. I knew I had to get them both back as soon as possible. Everything felt like a blur, and I was just going through the motions.

The relentless onslaught of rumors and accusations from my husband's family added an unbearable weight to my already heavy burden of grief. Their baseless fabrication, suggesting my involvement in my husband's passing, struck me like a betrayal of trust and love. Despite the emotional turmoil, I clung to the unwavering truth of my love for him, a bond that transcended the confines of earthly separation.

Amidst the chaos, the arrival of supportive relatives offered a semblance of solace and practical assistance in navigating the daunting task of making funeral arrangements. With their aid, I reached out to a trusted friend who owned a funeral home, entrusting him with the solemn responsibility of caring for my husband's remains and orchestrating the funeral proceedings. The paperwork and formalities that followed served as somber reminders of the irreversible reality of his passing.

> **Narcissists Grand Finale**
>
> This is a term used to describe an over-the-top ending of a relationship with a narcissist which is often characterized by an extreme amount of drama, chaos, lies, and overall outrageous, soap-opera type of behavior

Grief-stricken days, I maintained a strained yet necessary communication with one of my husbands' siblings, who had extended a helping hand by transporting one of our children from college. Despite the familial ties, it was evident that our rapport was strained by unspoken tensions and unaddressed grievances. Yet, amidst the fraught emotions and strained relationships, his presence offered a glimmer of reassurance in an otherwise tumultuous time. Through tearful conversations and weary exchanges, I found solace in the shared burden of mourning, clinging to the fragile threads of familial support amid the storm of grief.

> **Narcissists Grand Finale**
>
> The narcissist will blame their victim for their own bad behavior and then spread the lies far and wide to anyone who will listen, the true victim gets abused by people, while the narcissist plays the victim of being totally innocent, the villain plays the victim so well

The painful conversation with my husband's mother only deepened the wounds left by his passing. Her recounting of his final moments, filled with accusations and false allegations, added another layer of anguish to my already shattered heart. In her grief, she clung to a distorted narrative that painted me as the villain, blind to the truth that lay buried beneath layers of hurt and misunderstanding.

I found myself grappling with a torrent of unanswered questions, each one a poignant reminder of the complexities of our relationship and the painful truths that lay buried beneath the surface. If my husband truly loved us as he professed, why did he succumb to deception and betrayal? Why did he choose to walk away, leaving behind a trail of broken promises and shattered dreams? The weight of these unanswered questions threatened to engulf me, yet amidst the turmoil, I found solace in the unwavering truth that God alone held the answers to the mysteries of the human heart.

In the face of unfounded accusations and bitter recriminations, I clung to the unwavering truth of my own innocence and integrity. Despite the pain and confusion that surrounded me, I refused to allow myself to be defined by the lies and falsehoods that others sought to propagate. My conscience was clear, and I took refuge in the knowledge that God alone could judge the truth of my actions and intentions.

As I navigated the tumultuous aftermath of my husband's passing, I found strength in the unyielding love of my family and the unwavering support of those who stood by my side. Though the road ahead was fraught with uncertainty and pain, I resolved to face each new challenge with courage and resilience, trusting in the promise of healing and redemption that lay beyond the grief and loss.

The revelation of the malicious lies spread by my husband sent shockwaves through my world, shattering whatever remnants of trust and security remained. The depths of his deception and betrayal were staggering, leaving me reeling in disbelief and despair. As the truth emerged, it became painfully clear that I had become the target of a calculated smear campaign, engineered to tarnish my reputation and defame my character.

The venomous rumors, fueled by falsehoods and fueled by

> **Narcissists Weapon of Choice**
>
> A narcissist's weapon of choice is often verbal - slander, lies, playing the victim in flipped tales of who was the victim and who was the abuser, gossip, rage, verbal abuse, and intentional infliction of emotional pain. It is systematic dismantling of another person's relationships, reputation, emotional, spiritual, and physical health. This is why narcissists are often called "emotional vampires."

malice, spread like wildfire, engulfing me in a maelstrom of suspicion and distrust. In the insular confines of our small town, gossip became gospel, and I found myself cast as the villain in a narrative spun from deceit and manipulation. The weight of the accusations bore down on me, suffocating me with their insidious poison and leaving me isolated and alone.

To add insult to injury, some members of my husband's family chose to become willing accomplices in his campaign of character assassination, lending their voices to the chorus of condemnation that echoed through the community. Their betrayal cut me to the core, leaving me grappling with feelings of abandonment and betrayal. In their blind loyalty to my husband, they turned their backs on the truth, choosing instead to perpetuate the lies that threatened to consume me.

> **Narcissists Friends**
>
> Narcissists only surround themselves with people who enable their behavior or encourage their behavior. Anyone who tries to hold them accountable will be accused and blamed of the exact things the narcissists are guilty of. And the people who know the truth will remain silent.

As the walls of suspicion closed in around me, I found myself engulfed in a maelstrom of pain and betrayal, struggling to discern friend from foe in a world turned upside down by deceit and deception. Yet, amidst the darkness that threatened to engulf me, I clung to the flickering flame of hope, trusting that the truth would eventually emerge from the shadows and set me free from the web of lies that ensnared me.

The torrent of lies and slander unleashed by my husband's relatives was nothing short of bewildering and heartbreaking. It seemed as though they were on a crusade to paint me as a malevolent figure, weaving a web of deceit and falsehoods that cast me as the villain in my husband's tragic demise. The accusations hurled against me were as ludicrous as they were baseless, with wild claims of financial manipulation and even murder swirling in the toxic rumor mill.

The sheer volume of lies propagated by these individuals was staggering, leaving me reeling in disbelief and despair. It was as if they were grasping at straws, fabricating ever more outlandish tales in a desperate bid to tarnish my name and reputation. Their relentless campaign of character assassination spared no detail, with accusations ranging from financial malfeasance to cold-blooded murder.

> **Narcissists Families**
>
> It is very common for toxic family members to do a smear campaign in an attempt to scapegoat a survivor. Example: A toxic person will spin a survivor's words and actions to make it look like the victim was intentionally trying to cause problems in the family. In reality, the toxic person manipulated the entire situation in order to isolate the victim from other people.

As the rumors spread like wildfire, fueled by malice and vindictiveness, I found myself facing an onslaught of hostility and suspicion from those who had once been my family. The betrayal I felt was profound, as I watched in disbelief as individuals I had known for over 25 years turned against me with a ferocity that was both shocking and disheartening.

In the midst of the lies and deception, I couldn't help but wonder how people I had once considered family could stoop to such depths of cruelty and betrayal. It was a painful reminder that sometimes the bonds of blood are no match for the corrosive power of envy and greed. As the walls of suspicion closed in around me, I was left to confront the harsh reality that sometimes the greatest threats to our well-being can come from those closest to us.

The events that unfolded after my husband's passing were surreal and filled with hostility from several of his family members. Despite my attempts to seek reconciliation and cooperation, I was met with suspicion, hostility, and baseless accusations. It seemed that every effort I made to extend an olive branch was met with further animosity and resistance.

One particular incident stands out, when I attempted to visit my husband's family to discuss funeral arrangements and clear the air. Instead of finding a receptive audience, I was met with threats and accusations, culminating in a shocking call from one of my husband's siblings, who threatened to involve law enforcement based on unfounded allegations.

The level of hostility and paranoia displayed by my husband's family members was both bewildering and distressing. Despite my efforts to maintain civility and cooperation, they seemed determined to cast me as the villain in their narrative.

Throughout it all, I remained steadfast in my resolve to honor my husband's wishes and ensure that his final arrangements were carried out according to his desires. Despite the obstacles and hostility, I faced, I refused to compromise on what I knew to be his wishes, even in the face of opposition from his family.

In the end, I was left feeling saddened and disillusioned by the actions of those who should have been sources of support and comfort during such a difficult time. Instead, their actions only served to deepen the rift between us, leaving me to navigate the grief and uncertainty of my husband's passing alone.

Later that same day, one of my husband's relatives reached out to express sympathy for my situation as a young widow. However, she insisted that I involve my husband's sister and mother in the funeral arrangements. Despite my previous attempts to include them, they had warned me against involving the police. Despite my efforts, his family spread the false narrative that I didn't want their assistance. How could I desire their help after they had already threatened me? It became clear they weren't interested in offering genuine support; rather, they sought control. This experience taught me that when people can't control you, they resort to fabricating accusations.

Another call came from one of my husband's friends' spouses. She relayed that my husband's sister had contacted her, claiming I didn't want their involvement in the funeral arrangements. Perplexed by the situation, she urged me to reach out to them to resolve the issue. Similarly, they reached out to several others, spreading the false notion that I rejected their assistance. Yet, they never attempted to contact me directly, despite knowing my contact details and where I lived. Instead of reaching out to me, they expended effort contacting people from three different states. It seemed they were trying to paint me as the one blocking them, while in reality, they only sought involvement on their terms. It was evident they wanted control. Despite our shared pain, they not only misrepresented me but also sought to tarnish my reputation. They attempted to undermine my character and everything I stood for. In that moment, they became my adversaries.

In the late evening of the same day, a knock was heard at my door. To my surprise, it was the local sheriff's office. He asked to communicate with Mrs. Dyson, but since there were three Mrs. Dysons, I requested him to be more precise, to which he gave my name. He said that a female had been persistently calling the sheriff's office all day stating she was looking for my husband and that I wasn't responding to any of her calls. I asked the officer who the person was, and he gave me a name I hadn't heard before. I inquired if he had her contact number and he returned to his car to get it. After taking the phone, I called the number and asked to speak to the lady. I explained who I was, and the officer took the phone. He identified himself to the woman, saying she had called the station. Immediately, the call was disconnected. The officer attempted to call the number again. He turned to me and apologized stating he knew the lady's story didn't make sense, but he had to come to do a welfare check due to the multiple calls. He expressed his sympathy before departing.

When I reentered my home from the encounter with the officer, it all came flooding in; the death of my husband, the lies being told about me, the hostile behavior of his family, people slandering my name, and now this. I was overcome with emotion, sobbing, and screaming like never before, my family must have thought I was going mad. It was too much for me to handle. I had never experienced anything even close to this. It seemed like my world was turned upside down. It felt like I was in a bad dream, that I wanted to be awakened from. The Bible says God would not put more on you than you can handle. I didn't feel I could take any more nor did I want to. I wanted to shut myself off from the world.

The events of that day left me utterly speechless and in deep shock. I still couldn't wrap my mind around the sheriff's visit. I didn't even know what to think. Was my husband living a double life? All this time, I thought I knew him well, but it seemed like I didn't know him at all.

> **Double Life**
>
> Narcissists often lead a double life by maintaining a façade of stability and commitment publicly while secretly engaging in multiple relationships, using deceit and charm to manipulate and exploit their partners.

Wrapped up in a whirlwind of emotions and questions I wondered, was my husband keeping a dark secret from me? How could he betray me? Why else would a woman unknown to me would go out of her way to call the police all day attempting to find out information about him? All of a sudden, I felt so foolish and embarrassed. I was so naive to think that I knew my husband, while he was possibly living a secret life behind my back.

> **Pathological Lying**
>
> The term for this type of narcissistic behavior is "pathological lying" or "narcissistic infidelity." Pathological lying involves a consistent pattern of deceit, while narcissistic infidelity refers to the narcissist's tendency to engage in multiple relationships or affairs, often driven by a need for admiration, validation, and control.

I was angry and hurt. I was betrayed and deceived. I felt so used, like I had been taken advantage of, but I was also determined to get to the bottom of what was going on. I needed to know the truth. I had to find out all the details and figure out why he had kept this from me.

The truth was the woman who called the police station throughout the day was more than friends with my husband. The two had apparently been in a relationship for fifteen years. After contacting her, she revealed this bit of information that I was in the dark about. I knew I was legally his wife, but I felt lower than that of a side chick. How is it that she knew me, and where I lived but I knew nothing about her?

Even on the night of his passing, I received a friend request from an unfamiliar individual, whose name I recognized from previous encounters. I suspected she might have been someone from my husband's past. Hastily, I checked her Facebook profile and noticed she was connected to my husband and some of his relatives. I pondered why she would send me a friend request.

It struck me that she resided in the same area where my son had seen the parking pass in my husband's car, as indicated on her profile. Could she be another woman he was involved with? I considered the possibility that she might have called his phone, and when the authorities answered, they directed her to contact his wife. Perhaps that's why she sent me a friend request—to inquire about what had happened. I recalled the investigator mentioning they had my husband's phone when my son called. They chose not to answer it and inform him of the news. It's plausible that they responded to other calls that night and advised the callers to reach out to me.

I had hoped that things would calm down, but instead, they seemed to escalate. The phone calls I received weren't what I expected. Recently, a friend of my husband reached out, asking for a number that was stored in my husband's phone. To clarify, despite being told by the police that I could retrieve my husband's belongings after the investigation, I couldn't do so because his sister and mother had taken them before I could. Among those possessions was his bag, containing his wallet, keys, cell phone, and clothes. The phone that was taken along with the rest of his belongings was his work phone, not his personal one. When I went to the police station to collect his items, I was informed that someone else had already taken them.

I insisted on collecting my husband's belongings from the investigator. However, I was informed that his sister had already taken them. When I contacted her to inquire, she denied having the items and insisted that his wife needed to collect them. I relayed this information to the custodian at the police station, who went to verify. Upon her return, she presented me with a clipboard bearing my husband's sister's signature and identification number. It was clear that she had indeed collected the belongings. I couldn't understand why she would lie about it. The evidence was right in front of me. It was becoming increasingly apparent that this family was deceitful and manipulative.

I wondered how much more of this I could endure. My husband's workplace requested that I collect his belongings from his truck. Accompanied by my brother and one of my sons, they went to his workplace to retrieve his possessions. Upon their return, they found my husband's cellphone, indicating that his sister had taken the work phone, which his job needed back. My son provided them with his sister's number to retrieve the phone. She was furious to discover that she only had the work phone, not the personal one. What was the reason she sought his belongings? Was there something she didn't want me to look at or obtain access to?

She called my husband's friend to inform him I had the phone. He called me because he wanted some numbers from his phone. I told him I couldn't because the phone was locked. So, he asked me to try unlocking the phone. He went through a cycle of combinations to assist in unlocking it. He told me the numbers he was searching for. I told him to locate those people by some other method. His response was they weren't on social media. What was my husband's sister involvement in all this? Why was she so concerned? There were a lot of things I was unaware of or blatantly kept in the dark about. I didn't want to be informed. I took the phone, asked my son to power it off, and put it in a drawer. I couldn't handle it.

The following day, some of my husband's former coworkers came to offer their condolences, a gesture I deeply appreciated. One of them recounted an encounter with my husband, where they had tried to convince him to return home. He mentioned hearing me on the radio, expressing my love and forgiveness, emphasizing that I needed him back. Despite this, my husband remained adamant, convinced of my infidelity or wanting others to believe so. In a surprising revelation, the coworker mentioned that my husband had even gone as far as putting a tracker on my car. It seemed he was determined to ensure our paths wouldn't cross.

Over the next few days, I had to coordinate with the funeral home to finalize the arrangements. Unfortunately, the funeral home director was out of town for an event and wouldn't return for a few days. This news left me furious, but there was little I could do. In the meantime, I began packing my belongings and those of the children, as the funeral would be held in South Carolina. Additionally, one of my husband's colleagues started a GoFundMe campaign for me. Only close family members knew that I didn't have an insurance policy for my husband. The only financial assistance I had at the time was a union burial fund totaling $13,500, payable after the funeral. Therefore, I hoped the GoFundMe campaign would raise enough money to cover some of the funeral expenses.

Despite the assertion that I was well-funded by insurance, which wasn't the case. In June of that year, we met with an insurance representative to secure coverage for everyone, and though I was insured through my job, it didn't cover the family. A few days later, I learned that, based on their regulations, they were unable to provide the coverage we were requesting. The agent offered to research alternative companies. I said I'd search on my own, yet I didn't get the opportunity, since my spouse passed away six months later. Hence, my financial resources were limited. Even with the burial fund, I had to pay the funeral fees in advance, and I was uncertain where the money was going to come from. All I could do was take it one step at a time.

The undertaker had arranged a meeting for me at his office. We packed our automobiles in anticipation for the trip to South Carolina immediately after. During the meeting, I stated my desire to have the corpse shipped to our hometown and that it all had to be accomplished before the 13th of December, the date I had decided upon for the funeral.

Beforehand, I had contacted the funeral home in South Carolina where my aunt was the director. She gave explicit directions on what had to be done. In the office, we checked the legal records; I was assigned to bring some items to prepare the body for transport. Also, the fee for the funeral home services before transportation was almost six thousand dollars, coupled with the airline tickets. Through GoFundMe, we almost had enough. My family contributed the remaining amount. We were finally ready to go to South Carolina.

8

BETRAYAL AND REDEMPTION

In the last few days after my husband's demise, I could not bring myself to eat. Nothing seemed to entice me, and I was inundated with all the talk about things I had not done. Upon arriving in South Carolina, I was met with curious gazes. A few people contacted me to provide tidbits about what my husband's family had been saying. Little did they know that in a small town, anything shared was heard by everybody. I was then told about the rumors that I had contributed to his death, been unfaithful, taken advantage of him, and that we were now divorced.

My peace was shattered by the fact that instead of grieving, some of my husband's family were causing discord. They were worried about the wrong things. How is it? They were more concerned about what money they thought I had or was coming to me. Everyone who contacted me relayed the same tale of how I was supposed to have an exorbitant amount of insurance money. I was perplexed as to where it was since I had no clue about it. Furthermore, everyone was discussing me but not talking to me. They were preoccupied with all matters of no concern to them, but no one tried to assist with the funeral arrangements. It was their beloved, my husband, and the father of my children, yet they were not bothered about helping me. All I experienced was lies, deceit, persecution, and betrayal.

To add to the complexity, I received a call from someone I had heard was once involved in occult practices – a cousin of my husband. She offered condolences but also insinuated that I wasn't grieving. At the time, I was at the floral store selecting a casket spread and flowers. She proceeded to mention that she would inform a pastor she knew about my husband's passing. Unbeknownst to her, the person she referenced was one of my closest friends. True to her word, she contacted my friend and relayed numerous falsehoods about me. Some truths were mixed in, such as my poor credit, but she embellished further, claiming that my house belonged to my husband's sister and her husband, and that I possessed nothing. According to her, my husband had purchased our house and furnished it using a considerable inheritance from their father's passing, making his sister the rightful owner. The fabrications seemed endless, leaving me astounded at how people seemed to know the intimate details of my life, as if they resided with me. The web of lies seemed orchestrated by a select few individuals, and unfortunately, matters did not improve with time.

The remains of my husband arrived in South Carolina just a couple of days before the memorial service. Thankfully, my aunt took charge of all the arrangements. We discussed the paperwork and funeral plans a few times, and I couldn't help but feel like the Lord was guiding us through it all. Remarkably, my aunt managed to finalize everything without me having to spend a single cent. She reassured me not to worry about the expenses and mentioned that I could reimburse her whenever possible. However, I still had to handle the costs associated with the church service since my husband wasn't a member. This amounted to three thousand dollars. Altogether, the funeral expenses in South Carolina totaled around ten thousand dollars, with my family generously covering the remaining bills.

How is it possible that even in the midst of mourning, people can be insensitive and downright disrespectful? A few women contacted the funeral home, hoping to get a glimpse of my husband's remains. My aunt told them that they would not be allowed in until I had given my consent. They inquired again and again and were firmly refused by my aunt. These women weren't family; instead, I was told they had been romantically involved with my husband. As time passed, one after another, women emerged, claiming to have been in a relationship with him. Given that the time between his departure from me and his passing was only two and a half months, I couldn't fathom how he could have been romantically involved with all these women.

The day of the funeral arrived. Anticipating potential issues, I instructed my aunt to arrange for police presence due to concerns about one of my husband's sisters. The procession began at the home of a close relative of my husband. When organizing who would accompany my kids and me in the cars, I found that only three people from his family were willing to join; the others backed out. Despite the watchful eyes of family members filled with suspicion, I felt numb at that moment, just wanting the day to be over.

On that gloomy, wet day, we pulled up to the church. Through the car windows, I glimpsed the vibrant hues of orange and brown leaves adorning the trees. As we queued up to enter the church, I observed the usual arrangement: close family members, including spouses, children, parents, siblings, aunts, uncles, and so forth, would typically walk in together. But for me, it was just my children, myself, and a few of my family members and his cousins who made our way inside. The rest of his family sat at the back of the church. It felt incredibly disheartening.

As my sons and I found our seats, I watched as other family members approached the casket to pay their respects. Many passed by me without a word, some rolling their eyes or simply ignoring me. A few shook my children's hands in a show of acknowledgment.

As the service commenced, the casket was closed. Once again, my children and I waited for my husband's mother to join us, but she was conspicuously absent from her eldest son's farewell. None of his siblings from his mother's side, except his brother, were listed on the program, and one of his adopted sisters was present. The absence of the rest felt dishonorable. Nonetheless, the service proceeded beautifully until the near the end.

Towards the rear of the church, one of my husband's sisters, the root of all the turmoil, raised her voice to proclaim her brother's supposed happiness with is life. She went on to mention his plans to start his own business and his alleged joy after divorcing me. Her words caused an uproar in the church, prompting my son, brother, and some of the church trustees to escort her out. Surprisingly, most of her family followed her lead. With the police already on standby, I sat there, feeling overwhelmed. Apologies were offered for the disruptive incident, and the preacher, assisted by others, hastened to conclude the service. My husband's body and a few floral arrangements were removed, marking the end of the service due to the rain outside making the grounds wet.

The repast began, with food being served. Despite my readiness to leave, I maintained my composure, acknowledging people and expressing gratitude for their presence. Many offered condolences, admiring my perceived strength. Yet, I didn't want to be praised for strength; I was in pain. No one could truly understand the depth of my suffering. While outwardly, I seemed composed, internally, I was in agony. Did they realize the pain of knowing this was the last time I would see my husband on this side? Did they grasp the anguish for my children, now fatherless? Did they understand the hurt of betrayal, persecution, lies, and deceit? Did they sense the absence of my husband's mother and other family members at the funeral? Were they aware of the public humiliation and embarrassment? Did they comprehend the agony of being a victim of narcissistic abuse, not just from my late husband, but from several of his family members?

In the church dining hall, there was an individual who considered himself part of my husband's family, but to me, he seemed more like a foe. Unbeknownst to him, I was aware of the malicious gossip he was spreading. He seemed to have the ear of other family members, though I couldn't discern the source of his information. He consistently spread lies about me to anyone who would listen. Even after the funeral, he continued his campaign of falsehoods, echoing the same accusations as my husband's sister. According to him, I was unfaithful to my husband and portrayed myself as a terrible person. He even went as far as suggesting that the car I had been blessed with was purchased by my boyfriend. While a few people challenged his claims, most seemed eager to indulge in gossip, perpetuating negativity. It was disheartening to witness.

That night after the funeral, my youngest son received a distressing phone call from his grandmother and aunt. They informed him that his dad intended to take him away from me and offered him the option to live with them instead. This news left my son in tears, and he woke me up to share his anguish, expressing his desire to remain with me. I reassured him that no one would separate us, and eventually, he fell asleep.

Meanwhile, I was filled with anger and disbelief. How could his grandmother, who couldn't even attend her own son's funeral, have the audacity to disturb my son after we had just laid his dad to rest? It was a display of insensitivity and absurdity. I recalled the uncle's claim at the funeral that his mom couldn't attend due to her battle with cancer. If she was truly in such a condition, why would she call my child – her own grandchild – and attempt to disrupt his relationship with his mother? It was a glaring contradiction, and I couldn't comprehend their actions. If the roles were reversed, I doubt she would have appreciated such interference.

The next day, my sons and I set out on our journey home. I was exhausted, and I yearned to be home. As we stepped across the threshold of our house, there was a feeling of respite and a sentiment of desolation. Desolation in the sense that I would never see my spouse again; regardless of how things concluded, I still cherished him. He had been a part of my life for 25 years. Now, I had to readjust to a new lifestyle, cognizant that he wouldn't drop by or if I required something fixed, I couldn't phone him. Perhaps God was preparing me from the beginning. My grieving started way before his death.

When we returned home, I sat my kids down for a serious family discussion about their dad's demise, his adoration for them, and the way that things would be different moving forward. With everything that had occurred with their relatives, I clarified to them that I needed them to briefly suspend all correspondence with them for a brief timeframe. I needed time to think and breathe away from the eyes of anyone.

Before I blocked their numbers, my second most seasoned child connected with one of his dad's sisters to talk; however, I requested that he didn't do that. I figured he needed to understand why she acted like she did. I don't know what was said other than her accusing me of having something to do with her sibling's passing, and she advised him to pause and wait for the post-mortem report as it would uncover the real story. My child didn't tell me any further subtleties concerning that call.

We proceeded onward with our new life without their dad.

As Christmas approached, I was not content to remain in Maryland - only a couple of weeks had passed since we had buried my husband. I decided to visit my brother and his family in North Carolina. Only my family and two outsiders knew of our Christmas plans. It was a refreshing change of scenery, but when we returned home, I had the distinct feeling that someone had been in our residence. My children thought I was imagining things, yet I could detect a different scent in the air, one that was not usually present when I am away for a day. Additionally, there were no signs of any unwarranted entry, and nothing had been damaged, but I knew something was wrong.

We inspected the area; everything appeared to be in order, but I couldn't confidently state everything was in order. In my kitchen was an aisle in the center with drawers. I had stored some critical documents in one of the drawers for filing. These documents included my marriage certificate, past income tax records, and some additional miscellaneous items. Surprisingly, my marriage certificate was missing. I had a back-up, but my primary license had disappeared. Why would somebody enter my house and take my marriage certificate, of all things? I also noticed a few other items were gone. I didn't want the children to think I was going crazy, so I put the thought aside.

Not even a week later, I went back to work. Suddenly, the bank informed me that an effort to make a purchase worth three thousand dollars was made. At the same time, Verizon contacted me inquiring if I was buying numerous iPhones to be delivered to an address in New York. In addition, someone tried to open an Affirm account or complete a purchase through the same. All these events occurred at nearly the same time. Was this a coincidence? I do not believe so. The intruder had taken my confidential personal data. I was now a target of identity theft. The bank and Verizon aided me in launching a case. Simultaneously, similar occurrences began to take place with my kids associated with their bank accounts, email accounts and other accounts with their names. Whoever was behind this wanted to cause much damage.

For several months, an individual(s) had gained access to my email and LinkedIn accounts, as well as making multiple attempts to infiltrate my Facebook account. In my email account, more than one person was going through my emails without my knowledge until I started receiving notifications. I had made attempts to change the password quite often, but nothing was working. After contacting Microsoft, I was given instructions to keep track of the history of my account to discover the approximate area of the individual(s) responsible for this. As I followed the instructions, I was able to gain access to the timeline of my account. Surprisingly, the whereabouts of the perpetrator(s) were detected.

I was presented with an IP address and location of the same city and state where my husband's family resided and a few more locations I recognized. Unfortunately, I was not given a name, however, I was provided with the data about a certain city and the type of computing device the individual was using. Additionally, I was informed that a person from my home state had accessed my LinkedIn account. I had all the facts, and I could have shared them with the police, as I was encouraged to do. However, I experienced a strong feeling that God was telling me that vengeance was His, not mine.

Regardless of how much I wanted to file a report, I felt the Lord telling me not to. I couldn't comprehend why this was happening, especially when I had already faced so much. Unfortunately, all the lies my late husband told everyone and his "flying monkeys" made it impossible for me to take action. Despite the hurt of almost everyone turning their backs on my children and me, I could only trust in God. I prayed Psalm 64:

> *For the director of music. A psalm of David.*
>
> *<u>1</u> Hear me, my God, as I voice my complaint; protect my life from the threat of the enemy.*
>
> *<u>2</u> Hide me from the conspiracy of the wicked, from the plots of evildoers.*
>
> *<u>3</u> They sharpen their tongues like swords and aim cruel words like deadly arrows.*
>
> *<u>4</u> They shoot from ambush at the innocent; they shoot suddenly, without fear.*
>
> *<u>5</u> They encourage each other in evil plans, they talk about hiding their snares; they say, "Who will see it?"*
>
> *<u>6</u> They plot injustice and say, "We have devised a perfect plan!" Surely the human mind and heart are cunning.*
>
> *<u>7</u> But God will shoot them with his arrows; they will suddenly be struck down.*
>
> *<u>8</u> He will turn their own tongues against them and bring them to ruin; all who see them will shake their heads in scorn.*

> **9** *All people will fear; they will proclaim the works of God and ponder what he has done.*
>
> **10** *The righteous will rejoice in the LORD and take refuge in him; all the upright in heart will glory in him!*

As I grappled with the aftermath of identity theft and struggled to regain a sense of normalcy, I found myself in a place where trust was hard to come by. The betrayal, persecution, and lies propagated by those I once considered family left me feeling isolated. In order to protect myself and my family, we made the difficult decision to cut off contact with many individuals associated with my husband. This was necessary to shield ourselves from ongoing emotional abuse and turmoil. Already grappling with Post Traumatic Stress Disorder (PTSD), I couldn't afford to subject myself to further distress.

Some individuals connected to my husband seemed to be monitoring us or exhibiting a monitoring spirit, gathering information to relay back to others. Some distorted the truth, while others added embellishments, further fueling the false narratives being spread about me. This only served to divert attention away from the real truth, which many were working hard to conceal in order to preserve their own reputations and avoid accountability for their actions.

To compound matters, I received apologies from a few individuals who acknowledged their absence as friends during my ordeal. One person, a childhood friend residing just over an hour away, shared a troubling encounter he had with my late husband at a casino one night.

During his visit, he observed his cousin dining with my husband, leading him to suspect they were romantically involved. Uncertain about the duration of their relationship, he confronted his cousin as they left the casino. Upon questioning my husband's marital status, he was told they were separated. Curious, he inquired about the wife's identity, and to his surprise, it was mine. Recalling our connection from school, he sensed something was amiss. His cousin assured him my husband had claimed to be single, despite her knowledge of our marriage. She recounted a recent conversation where she overheard me questioning my husband's phone calls. This revelation left my friend feeling regretful for not informing me sooner. In response, I reassured him that he bore no responsibility for the situation.

Yet again, I was told that my husband was engaged in an extramarital affair. With this, I decided to go through my late husband's possessions that we still owned, plus the stuff from his job, which was in the company's vehicle. There were some garments as well as his work boots, a heap of papers, private devices and instruments, and other miscellaneous items. I took a garbage bag to get rid of the unnecessary articles. Here I was going through his last belongings, and not surprisingly, in his work boots were condoms and male enhancement pills. I chucked them all into the trash. Going through the papers was quite straightforward. Most of the papers were accounts with his name on them.

Nevertheless, I came across a receipt from a pawn shop where he pawned his wedding ring, one of my bracelets, and my necklace. For each, he received no more than one hundred and fifty dollars. After seeing this, I was disheartened and thought to myself, for him to pawn these items he must have needed some quick money. I guess this was the time to stop being disappointed. I was coming to the realization of who he was or the person he became before his death. But then again, he was this person all along. He was a master of deception and manipulation. The mask had fallen.

At the far left-hand side of the garage, there were some more items I needed to get rid of. Concealed in the corner were alcohol containers, the majority of them were already drained, in conjunction with cigars, and other miscellaneous objects. All of them were thrown away.

I was completely drained but I still wanted to finish the task. I re-entered the house and made my way to his junk drawer. It was full of papers and various other items. I took everything out and started to read through each document one by one. His bank statements were also included in the pile. To my amazement, there were quite a few Cash App transactions made to females ranging from twenty to one hundred dollars. I noticed recurrent deductions from his account to a few familiar names.

Over a span of a few months, thousands of dollars had been sent to various women. One of the names was from our hometown; money was sent to her every other day. Others were given money on a weekly basis. Then I noticed the name of someone from New York, who I knew of; she was supposedly a long-time friend's ex-girlfriend, and another person from Miami, Florida, whose identity was not known. Immediately, I thought that maybe the person he was sending money to in New York was the same person he had an extramarital affair with.

Some of the women he sent money to were friends with me on Facebook – liking and commenting on my content. To be honest, this may sound crazy, but I had nothing against them even though they may have thought I wasn't aware of their interactions and transactions with my husband. They too were a part of his grand scheme and web of lies. He lied to everyone, it didn't matter if you were his friend, family, co-worker, or acquaintance. His lies were his truths in his mind; otherwise known as "False Sense of Reality.". In actuality, his lies were his actual admissions.

I was continuously learning that my late husband was a deceiver, a swindler, and a fraud. It all made sense. The explanation for why his money was never shown or why I was oblivious of it, was because he was providing for other women. How could he take from his own home, leading to our financial difficulties? There he was taking care of not two or three, but five women. God does not accept wrongdoings and that saying holds true that whatever is done in secrecy will eventually be exposed.

I had come to the point where I needed to inform the lawyer of my husband's demise. She asked me a few questions and mentioned that she would present the papers to the court to drop the divorce case. After a couple of days, she returned to me, inquiring if I was aware of any kids my husband might have had. I replied in the negative and asked why she was repeating the same question she'd asked before.

She said when she went to the court to file the forms, someone by the name of Megan had submitted a document as an interested party in the divorce case. My attorney furthermore stated that the person had a PO Box address in a neighboring city, and she had an email address. She said she would mail a letter to that address to inquire, and I could do the same if I wanted. My email account was accessed from an IP address linked to the same area of the PO Box; now, the address of a person involved in the divorce case was from the same place. This was not a mere coincidence. This was someone familiar with the situation, with me, my husband, and all else taking place. I assumed this individual was a close relative of my husband.

A communication from a lawyer's office in a nearby town was sent to my husband which mentioned that on December 9th, 2019, a call or a visit had been made to their office for the proceedings of our divorce. This was utterly astonishing as he had already passed away on the 4th of December and was buried on the 13th. This conversation lasted for half an hour, which means that someone had gone in his stead to acquire further information on our case. But why? We had never moved forward to court and there was no set date. Could this person be looking for something that they felt belonged to them, like the house or his possessions?

I was made aware of so many facts I was oblivious to as it concerned my late husband. And still yet there was probably even more that I wasn't made aware of. I know that I serve a great God, and according to his word, He would make known things to a prophet. This is what He was doing, disclosing the adversary's plans, tricks, and stratagems. I hadn't understood that numerous people could dislike me. I could accept if I was in the wrong, but these allegations were all false. I remembered feeling so overburdened and pained.

I returned to church for the first time since I'd laid my husband to rest. While there, I recollected the pastor conveying these words of wisdom:

"You are not to blame for what happened. The things people are trying to place on you are not yours. They are trying to give you things that belong to them. It is taken off you this day. You will no longer carry other people's burdens. I see you moving; I can see you packing boxes. The Lord wants you to go even higher, Woman of God. There is another level for you. Your children needed to be here today to see you delivered from these things. The Lord says he has your children; you don't have to worry. I know what you have gone through, your writing, and even blogging about it. Your tears will turn into tears of joy. Where the Lord is moving you, you and your children will be happy and joyful in that new place. Where you're at, these people are trying to keep you bound. In your new place, you will thrive. The Lord sets you free today from those things people have spoken against you and your children. The curse is broken today. The Lord says rest. You will sleep at night. Also, your family is a millionaire. Your children will take care of you. All your children are mighty men of God. You will be fine. Your feet were anointed to take territory in the places the Lord is sending me."

From that day, I began to speak life and not death:

I am the head and not the tail; I am above and not beneath. I am blessed going in and coming out. I am anointed and appointed by the Father; I decree my healing spiritually and naturally. I decree increase in all areas of my life. I decree new opportunities coming my way. I decree divine connections. I decree I am flourishing in all areas of my life. I decree debt cancellation. I decree open doors. I decree fresh anointing/ new oil. I decree favor with our move. I decree favor with land, construction. I decree favor with the children's college fees. I decree their open doors/advancements. I decree favor in all areas of their lives. I decree prolific books written. I decree an uptick in sales. I decree prolific conferences and meetings. I decree the joy of the Lord is mine. I decree favor from the north, south, east, and west. I decree walking in my calling with boldness. I decree new spiritual eyes and ears. I decree newfound zeal for the Lord. I decree the heart of God is mine. I decree healing/blessed hands. I decree my feet are steadfast in the Lord. I decree my healing emotionally, physically, mentally, spiritually, financially, academically, and every other part of my life not mentioned.

I decree to be a friend to God like Abraham. I decree I am favored and have a business mind like Joseph. I decree favor like Queen Esther. I decree I am a builder like Nehemiah. I decree I am a prophet and judge like Deborah. I decree my latter shall be greater like Job. I decree by the blood of Jesus that I will possess territories like Jabez and Isaiah. I decree this is my season of acceleration and manifestation. I decree this is my breakout and banner year.

REVELATIONS AND REALIZATIONS: UNCOVERING THE TRUTH

For two months, I was overwhelmed with misery, suffering, and grief. I composed a letter to my late husband to articulate my feelings. Though he was not here to read it, this action was therapeutic for me. He had left me with unresolved issues. This was one of multiple letters I wrote to him.

March 28th, 2020
    A Letter To Rufus Bennett, Jr.

Hi Rufus,
  I know you're not here to read this letter, b/c I thought it would be fitting to write it considering you left with unfinished business. Maybe I shouldn't say unfinished business. Well, let me begin by saying I loved you with every ounce of my being, I gave birth to our 4 sons — Justin, Javon, Jordan, & Jonathan. I was there for you, stayed with you when the going was rough — I remained. I was there with you through thick & thin. We had good times & bad times. Since you left, I felt like I never knew you. I can't believe how you played me — how you told all those lies saying I was cheating on you for 15 years, when you & I know that wasn't the truth. In retrospect, it was you all alone who was cheating & lying. All the nights you left to go to the Casino or play pool & didn't return until the next day! I was so livid w/ you & asked you on multiple ocassions if you were cheating; you denied it; made me though I was crazy. You played Mr. Nice guy — all along neglecting your family. You would buy gifts b/c you felt that would smooth things over b/c of your indencres.

Oh, do you remember after we moved into our house — that business trip you went on & how you conveniently met some lady & had a one night stand? You came back home went to the doctor to get tested for STD's & I found the lab results. You couldn't hide that so you told me. Oh, how about the time I found a condom in your pants pocket & you made it seem like it wasn't yours. OR do you remember the time when we were on our way to church & it was a woman's umbrella in the car & you played crazy like you didn't know where it came from. How about the time when you would stop talking to me for no reason; I guess it was a form of punishment b/c I was on you too much.

The ultimate was when you left on Sep 22, 2019 out the blue saying you wasn't happy. You left me 2 going on 3 mortgage payments behind. You could have cared less b/c you was out. Man, you went around to everyone saying how I treated you so bad & how you did everything for me. But you forgot to tell them how you was never around, neglected your family, how you lied to justify your actions. But, I was the one!

You knew my every move, but for you to say those means things was the icing on the cake. I guess you had to make up something that people would believe. Right? So, why not tell them something that happened 15yrs ago & make it appear to be happening today. I must say you did it. Way to go. On top of that, you told everyone you came in contact with.

But, you fail to say I was there for you when you had recently lost your job in Aug 2019. Or how I was helping you or should I say I was starting up a business for you. Do you recall HVAC 365, then I made a mistake & put HVAC 360? Do you recall me sitting w/ you asking about what services you would offer in order for me to have flyers printed? Do you remember me doing your resume to get a job & how I prayed & went on a fast for you? Do you remember how I borrowed money from my 401k to make certain we had. How many times I did that? Countless w/o a problem until I felt you was taking advantage of me.

Do you recall Fall term 2019 when Justin & Jarron went back to college?

I'M NOT MAD AT YOU!

I'm not mad at you for trying to emotionally destroy me.
I'm not mad at you that I had to beg for the bare minimum.
I'm not mad at you for treating me like a second option.
I'm not mad at you for how you continued to do things
after I begged you to stop on a daily basis.
I'm not even mad at you for the things that happened any longer.
I was mad at myself for accepting your behavior and thinking
it was normal when I deserved nothing but the world.

But now,

I AM FREE!

I am free to take time to pause and reflect. I am free to listen to my inner voice and make decisive actions. I am free to forgive myself and let go of the past. I am free to be kind and compassionate to myself. I am free to be at peace with the present moment and not worry about the future.

I am free to set healthy boundaries and take responsibility for my emotional well-being. I am free to be authentic and express my feelings.

I am free to find joy in the little things that life has to offer. I am free to practice self-love and embrace my flaws. I am free to be the person I want to be and create the life I desire.

I am free to open my heart and accept the love that I deserve. I am free to embrace new opportunities that bring me closer to my dreams. I am free to let go of anything that no longer serves me and find my own unique path.

I am free to create the life I want for myself and make every day count. I am free to explore my creativity and express my authentic self.

I am free to be who I am and find joy in the journey. I am free to heal from the past and create a future full of potential.

I am free!

As time went on, I felt the presence of God urging me to move away. I no longer wanted to stay in the same area where the source of my trauma was located. Nothing was keeping me here, and my late husband's relatives and I were not in contact. As a way to mend broken fences, one of my youngest sons went to his relatives' church two months after his father's passing. Upon arrival, he was welcomed by some members of the family, but his grandmother and aunt were absent. When he asked the pastor for their address, he gave my son their phone numbers instead.

My son attempted to contact his grandmother, yet she never responded to his call. When he reached out to his aunt, she explained that she was too busy caring for two children to meet up with him. She asked who he was with. Oddly enough, when he returned from church, I received a text from her claiming that we were trying to murder them and would not get away with it. This was completely ridiculous. She even forwarded the message to other people. I believe she was losing her mind. My son had gone alone out of kindness. No one else had gone with him.

He showed maturity beyond his years and acted as if he was a grown man, and they were the children. I told him to stay away from them and let them suffer. You can't force someone to love you or talk to you, even if they're family. It was a valuable lesson. But I'm sure they would twist the story to make them seem like the victim.

After that encounter, my husband's aunts told me that she had seen my son in church and was overjoyed to meet him. She gave him some cash and interrogated whether I needed anything.

Honestly, I was in need; yet I didn't need her to realize it. I was grateful for the money she had given me. She said that everybody knew how her niece acted, in terms of her conduct. It wasn't the first occasion when she had demonstrated such behavior. I recounted to her aunt my distress and she said that her sister had never unveiled what transpired. She emphatically expressed that she didn't support others favoring her niece or overlooking my husband's activities. Amid the discussion, she proposed that I should keep on doing what God had commanded me to do and nor stress over the rest. It was a relief to hear this from her. I respected her and her husband, they were both upstanding Christians, if just others resembled them.

It had been almost five months since the death of my late husband. Until this point, I hadn't acquired the finished autopsy record. The underlying discoveries were inadequate. I couldn't move titles from his name to mine because I still required the report to document forms through Probate Court. I had a dream that the reason for his death was discovered to be PCP. After I stirred from the dream, I looked into PCP. It's normally known as Angel Dust or Molly. In some cases, it's mixed with Maryjane or in powder, fluid, or pill structure.

On May 15th, I was informed that the autopsy report was finalized, revealing the cause of death.

My dreams prior to my late husband's death were accurate; the analysis verifying his overindulgence in drugs. God had cautioned me by means of my visions, yet I was ignorant to the truth. I informed my sons regarding the findings, and they were startled to discover their father was consuming a drug of this nature. They were perplexed as to why he would take something resembling an aphrodisiac.

Several days later, I obtained the official report from the funeral home. I couldn't decide if I was feeling relieved or not. It was troubling to find out that my husband had passed away due to consuming an illegal drug, either for the purpose of getting high or a sex drug. I was not cognizant of him taking narcotics; I was only aware that he was a frequent marijuana smoker, but nothing else. Six months after my husband's death, the papers were settled in Probate Court for a Small Estate; I received the Letter of Administration granting me the right to transfer his vehicle's title. The mortgage was in both of our names, so there were no additional procedures I needed to take, other than continuing to pay it. Shortly after, I had another dream concerning him.

June 4, 2020

DREAM
In the early morning hours I had a VIVID dream about Rufus. In this dream we were in bed together + he was holding me tightly talking to me. I Recalled asking him about Heaven + how he was doing. He said he was really good + at peace where he was at. His smile was so bright + his complexion was clear. He appeared to be so happy.

As he was holding me I was telling him that I love him, I don't recall if he said he loved me. He said he will always be with us. He was saying other things, b/ the only other thing I Recalled is he was telling me about his sister children + how she called one of them "man". As he was telling me I thought to myself "now why is he telling me about her". I listened + as he was talking about her + the kids it brought so much joy to him. Shortly after the dream shifted to him telling me about a pharmacy being built in a small town called Rimini. This pharmacy was to be built down a dirt road. I thought that was strange. The weird thing even though I was dreaming that he was telling me; my sister in law was in the dream seem like telling me the exact thing. I was awaken from dream

10

EMBRACING CHANGE: FINDING HOME IN UNEXPECTED PLACES

I often think about my late husband. It gives me a sense of security to believe he is in a good place and at peace. I know he would have wanted our children and me to be content and at ease. There are still times when I can feel him in the room. I remember the first time I sensed My husband' presence after he passed. I was in the bathroom when I felt a strange yet calming aura, almost as if he were there with me. I stood still, wondering why he might be there or if I was imagining it.

Another time, I was lying in bed early one morning when I once again felt his presence. It seemed as though I was embraced in his arms while the song "Goodbye Love" by Guy played in a dream-like state. I soon woke up. Later that day, my curiosity led me to listen to the song's lyrics.

The song delves deeply into the anguish and turmoil of a relationship that is unraveling, vividly portraying the protagonist's emotional conflict as they confront the end of their love. Despite their deep-seated reluctance to leave and the profound sadness they feel, past heartbreak and temptation ultimately compel them to walk away. The lyrics express a sense of betrayal and guilt, highlighting how broken promises and shattered dreams have tainted the relationship. Phrases like "You said you'd never leave me, I said I'll never leave you" underscore the initial vows and mutual intentions to stay together, making the eventual separation feel like a poignant failure of their promises.

The second verse intensifies the emotional struggle, depicting the protagonist's bleak days and tearful moments without their partner. They grapple with feelings of guilt over their decision to leave, questioning whether it will make them appear foolish. The song captures their desperate longing for reconciliation, as they cling to hope and pray for their lover's return while feeling the weight of betrayal and self-reproach.

The outro poignantly encapsulates the protagonist's confusion and deep sorrow. The repetition of "goodbye" emphasizes the painful finality of their decision, underscoring the profound sense of loss and regret. The protagonist's plea for one more moment together reflects their overwhelming sadness and unresolved feelings, acknowledging that despite their desire to stay, they must ultimately accept the end of the relationship and the guilt that accompanies it.

Saying goodbye to our old life and welcoming new opportunities became paramount after my husband's death. The thought of moving to a new place, once a mere consideration, now felt urgent and necessary. I undertook a spiritual fast, seeking divine guidance for the right direction and a place where my boys could flourish. With time off work, I visited Atlanta, Georgia, exploring neighborhoods in South Atlanta and nearby areas. Although we explored several promising locations, none felt like the right fit. On our last day, I prayed earnestly, asking God to clear the path for us if it was His will for us to embrace a new beginning and start fresh in a new place.

While staying at the hotel, I was overcome by an inexplicable feeling that this place felt like home. I began searching for houses in the neighborhood, and a couple of my sons accompanied me to view the properties.

Eventually, I narrowed my choices down to two places. When I met with the real estate agent, she suggested I look at a display unit. I did, and I was smitten. The hardest part was the credit assessment. The agent called the bank to check my credit, and unbelievably, I received a pre-approval notice to acquire the house I wanted. I was ecstatic and knew this was God's doing. I entered into a contract with an anticipated closing date of November 18, 2020.

When I returned home, the work began; I phoned my church friend — the lawyer I had previously consulted — to chat. She was one of the most reputable in the region and I knew she would help to make this transition smooth. We met that week to examine the process and for me to decide if I wanted to contract with her. It didn't take long for me to come to a conclusion. I employed her, and we started the work.

I had four months to complete the sale of our residence. I got in touch with a neighboring contractor to repair minor issues around the house and then went through every room, disposing of certain items and giving away the rest. I gave away all of my husband's tools to a local, small-scale HVAC businessman. I did not want to go through the difficulty of listing those things for sale. Besides, the Lord blessed me in many ways; it was my opportunity to help someone else. The gentleman was so grateful for the gift.

I put the house up for sale and everything went well. We closed in November, and I officially left Maryland on November 13th to start a new life with new beginnings.

Isaiah 43:18-19
Forget the former things; do not dwell on the past. See I am doing a new thing! Now it springs up; do you not perceive it?

11

FIVE YEARS LATER

The past five years have been profoundly transformative. The aftermath of betrayal and narcissistic abuse has been an incredibly challenging journey, one that has tested my resilience and strength in ways I never anticipated. The process of healing required me to delve deeply into the complexities of narcissistic personality disorder (NPD), striving to find closure and regain a sense of normalcy in my life.

In my quest for understanding, I invested years in researching the behavioral traits and psychological mechanisms behind narcissism. This extensive research revealed a crucial truth: I was not alone in my suffering. Many others have experienced similar patterns of abuse and, like me, found themselves grappling with the realization of being victimized. The abuse I endured may not have left physical scars, but the emotional and mental wounds were profound and enduring. The subtlety of the abuse often meant that its impact was not immediately apparent, leaving many of us feeling isolated and confused.

Being entangled in a relationship with a narcissist can feel like an unending emotional rollercoaster. The highs and lows are intense and unpredictable, creating a sense of instability that can leave you feeling like you're trapped in a fog. The insidious nature of narcissistic abuse means that the damage is not always visible but is deeply embedded in your psyche. It often distorts your perception of reality, making it difficult to see the true nature of the situation while you're still in it.

It's only after you manage to extricate yourself from the abusive environment that the full extent of the damage becomes clear. The process of coming to terms with what you've experienced can be overwhelming, as the fog begins to lift and the clarity of your situation becomes more apparent. Understanding and processing these experiences often requires the guidance of mental health professionals who can help you navigate the complex emotions and psychological effects of narcissistic abuse. Their support can be instrumental in piecing together the fragments of your sense of self and finding a path toward healing and recovery.

Emerging from this experience, I have risen stronger, like a phoenix from the ashes—symbolizing rebirth and renewal. Through my healing journey, I sought professional help, delved deeply into self-discovery, and learned to embrace and love myself. I explored new interests, pursued advanced degrees, established healthy boundaries, and engaged in community service. Joining women empowerment organizations, nurturing genuine friendships, and allowing myself to be open to new chapters in life were all part of my growth. Most importantly, I worked on forgiving both those who hurt me and myself, which was a significant part of my healing.

You might wonder if I ever reconnected with those who betrayed me. Recently, a member of my husband's family reached out to offer an apology. This unexpected gesture opened a door to address the unresolved pain that had lingered in my heart.

In that conversation, I took the opportunity to openly express how their actions had profoundly affected me and my children. Verbalizing the impact of their behavior was an essential part of my healing journey. It allowed me to confront the hurt directly and share the emotional toll that had been taken on our lives. This exchange was not just about airing grievances; it was about giving voice to the suffering that had been silent for too long.

Although I had already forgiven them in my heart, having this external acknowledgment was a significant step toward closure. It was a validation of the pain I had endured and an affirmation of the healing process I had embarked upon. This reconciliation provided a sense of resolution, enabling me to move forward with a renewed sense of peace.

I firmly believe that everything unfolds according to God's plan. Forgiveness, while challenging, is a vital component of this process. It releases us from the chains of bitterness and rage, allowing us to heal and grow. By letting go of these burdens, we make room for new beginnings and a more hopeful outlook on life. Through forgiveness, we transform our own pain into a source of strength and resilience, empowering us to move past the hurt and embrace the future with a lighter heart.

What's Next For Me

I'm thrilled to share that I am currently working on two new books, each aimed at providing deeper insights and support for those who have endured the trials of narcissistic abuse.

The first book, *From Pain to Purpose: A Faith-Based Guide to Healing from Narcissism*, will offer an in-depth exploration of narcissistic personality disorder (NPD) and its impact on individuals. This guide will combine practical strategies with spiritual guidance, drawing on faith-based principles to help readers understand and navigate their healing journey. It will address the nuances of narcissistic behavior and offer faith-driven methods for recovery, empowering readers to find purpose and resilience in the aftermath of abuse.

Following this, I will be working on *Moving Past the Hurt: Reclaiming Your Identity*. This book will focus on the critical process of rebuilding and rediscovering your true self after experiencing abuse. It will provide practical tools and emotional support for those seeking to regain their sense of identity, restore self-esteem, and cultivate a life of fulfillment and authenticity. The goal is to help readers move beyond their pain and embrace their inner strength, paving the way for a renewed and empowered self.

I am deeply grateful for your support and involvement in this journey. Your engagement has been a source of encouragement and inspiration. As we continue to navigate these complex and transformative experiences, I look forward to sharing more insights and resources with you. Together, let's continue to grow, heal, and find strength in our faith.

CONCLUSION

In the world of loss, the end isn't a final stop but a way to new beginnings. Looking back on my life after my husband passed away, I'm amazed by how grief can change us. It transforms despair into hope, taking us from dark times to brighter days. Throughout this journey, I learned how strong the human spirit is. It's a spirit that can endure the toughest nights, find comfort in small joys, and build strength from broken dreams. This journey through loss has ultimately brought me to a place of renewed hope and resilience.

In this concluding chapter, I stand not just as someone who survived loss but as proof of the healing power of time, faith, and perseverance. The journey wasn't easy, and the pain of grief still lingers, reminding me of the love and presence I once had.

Despite this deep sorrow, I found unexpected sources of strength. I found comfort in the support of loved ones, in cherished memories, and in the guidance of faith. I learned the power of resilience, the importance of forgiveness, and the beauty of embracing life, even with its fragility.

As this chapter ends, it's not a goodbye to my husband because his memory still holds his lasting legacy. His life taught me about love, commitment, and the importance of cherishing each moment. He remains a part of my soul, guiding me as I move forward into new experiences.

To those who have shared this journey of grief with me, I offer my deepest sympathy and support. I hope this story serves as a sign of hope, showing that even in the darkest times, dawn eventually comes. Life, in its infinite wisdom, bestows upon us both joy and sorrow, love and loss. And within this paradox lies the sublime beauty of existence, the endless evolution of the human spirit, ever resilient, ever hopeful, and ever embracing life's intricate and unpredictable journey.

SOUNDTRACK TO MY JOURNEY

As I reflect on the journey chronicled in these pages, I realize how deeply music has intertwined with my experiences. Each song on this playlist holds a special significance, capturing the emotions, struggles, and triumphs I faced while surviving and healing from narcissistic abuse.

Here's a curated selection of songs that accompanied me through the darkest moments and helped me rise again:

"Fight Song" by Rachel Platten
A reminder to stay strong and fight for my own happiness, even when I felt like giving up.

"Stronger" by Kelly Clarkson
This anthem helped me embrace the strength I discovered within myself after enduring pain.

"Survivor" by Destiny's Child
A declaration of resilience, this song echoed my determination to rise above my circumstances.

"Praying" by Kesha
Its heartfelt lyrics resonated with my journey toward healing and self-empowerment.

"Rise Up" by Andra Day
A powerful anthem of hope, inspiring me to keep rising despite the setbacks.

"Unbreakable" by Alicia Keys
This song reminded me of my inner strength and the bonds I formed with those who supported me.

"Ex-Factor" by Lauryn Hill
A poignant exploration of love and heartache, reminding me of the complexities of relationships.

"Goodbye Love" by Guy
A reflection on letting go of love that no longer serves you.

"I'm Coming Out" by Diana Ross
An anthem of self-acceptance and embracing one's true self.

"Superwoman" by Alicia Keys
A powerful tribute to the strength and resilience of women.

"Rise Up" by Alita
A moving call to rise above challenges, reinforcing my journey of empowerment.

"She Is A Warrior" by Alita
Celebrating the strength of women, this song resonates with the fight within us all.

Gospel Songs

"Broken But I'm Healed" by Byron Cage
A reminder that healing is possible, even after deep pain

"Better" by Hezekiah Walker
This uplifting song encourages hope and the promise of better days ahead.

"Put It On The Altar" by Jessica Reedy
A heartfelt invitation to surrender burdens and seek healing.

"Something Out of Nothing" by Jessica Reedy
This song reminds us that we can create beauty from our struggles.

"Can't Give Up Now" by Mary Mary
An inspiring reminder to persevere through life's challenges.

"You Know My Name" by Tasha Cobbs-Leonard
A powerful affirmation of identity and faith in one's journey.

"Deliver Me" by Donald Lawrence
A plea for liberation from pain and the promise of freedom.

"You Don't Know My Story" by John P. Kee
A celebration of resilience and the unique journey each person faces.

How to Listen

I invite you to explore this playlist as you reflect on the themes of survival, healing, and empowerment in my story. You can find the playlist on YouTube-_Till Betrayal Do Us Part Playlist #1_ and _Till Betrayal Do Us Part Playlist #2_ or search for it by title. Let the music accompany your own journey of self-discovery and resilience.

Final Thoughts

Music has a unique ability to touch our hearts and inspire us, often saying what we can't articulate. As you listen to these songs, I hope you find strength in your own journey, knowing that healing is possible, and love is worth fighting for.

Thank you for joining me on this path. May you continue to embrace your own story with courage and grace.

APPENDIX

If you are in a relationship with a narcissist, recognize the signs so that you can protect yourself and your family.

5 Common Examples of Narcissists' Games

Narcissists may engage in various manipulative tactics to maintain control, manipulate emotions, and protect their fragile self-esteem. It's essential to be aware of these behaviors to recognize and address them. Here are some common examples of narcissistic games:

1. Silent Treatment
The narcissist may use the silent treatment as a way to punish their former partner for leaving them or as a means of expressing anger or resentment. This tactic involves ignoring or refusing to communicate with the ex-partner, leaving them confused, hurt, and excluded.

2. Gaslighting
The narcissist is breaking up with me, but they keep blaming me when I am not at fault. Gaslighting is a manipulative tactic where the narcissist distorts the truth or denies reality to make their partner doubt their memories, perceptions, and sanity.

During a breakup, the narcissist may use gaslighting to undermine the ex-partner's confidence and make them question the validity of their emotions and experiences.

According to **Dr. Jenni Jacobsen**, PhD, a psychology expert:

Gaslighting occurs when someone manipulates another person to the extent that the person begins to question their own reality. This is often achieved by downplaying the seriousness of abusive behavior. A gaslighter may say or do something cruel and then later tell the victim that it wasn't that serious and that the victim is just being too sensitive.

3. Triangulation

Triangulation involves the narcissist bringing a third person into the situation to hurt their ex-partner even more. By using the third person to make their ex feel inadequate, ugly, insecure, or jealous, the narcissist aims to show off a perceived "better" replacement and make their ex-partner feel worthless and irrelevant.

Triangulation might involve the narcissist beginning to date someone new and then telling their former partner that the new partner thinks the former partner is "crazy."

4. Hoovering

Hoovering is a tactic where the narcissist attempts to draw their ex-partner back into the relationship or engage in intermittent reinforcement to keep their ex emotionally invested.

It can involve professing love, displaying false remorse, or making promises of change to manipulate the ex-partner into reconsidering the breakup and returning to the narcissist's control.

5. Smear Campaign

During and after a breakup, the narcissist may engage in a smear campaign against their ex-partner. This involves spreading false information, rumors, or negative portrayals of the ex-partner to damage their reputation, isolate them from support networks, and maintain control over the relationship narrative.

It is important to note that these behaviors can significantly impact the ex-partner's mental and emotional well-being. Seeking support from friends, family, or a mental health professional can help navigate the aftermath of a relationship with a narcissistic individual.

5 Reasons Why Narcissists Play Breakup Games

A narcissist is a master manipulator, often charming, and someone who can get away with what they want. These are just some descriptions fit for a narcissist, but did you know that their biggest fear is being alone?

They thrive when someone loves them and gives them praise, attention, and admiration. Unfortunately, they cannot share the same feelings or emotions that their partner has for them..

Once a person with NPD realizes their partner wants to leave them, they opt for narcissistic mind games. They aim to confuse, cause guilt, and change the mind of their partners to make things work for them.

These narcissistic games or manipulation techniques will only make things worse for the victim. Narcissists look for a constant need for admiration and lack empathy for others. When it comes to relationships, narcissists may engage in breakup games or manipulative behaviors for various reasons.

It's important to note that not everyone who exhibits narcissistic traits engages in breakup games, and not all breakups involve manipulative behavior. However, for those with narcissistic tendencies, there are several reasons why they might engage in breakup games:

1. Power and Control

Narcissists thrive on having power and control over their partners. They can manipulate and control their partner's emotions and actions by playing breakup games. This allows them to maintain a sense of superiority and dominance in the relationship.

2. Attention-Seeking

Narcissists crave attention and validation from others. By playing breakup games, they can elicit strong emotional reactions from their partners, giving them the desired attention and validation. Their partner's emotional distress becomes a source of narcissistic supply for them.

3. Fear of Abandonment

Despite their self-centered behavior, narcissists often have deep-seated fears of abandonment. Playing breakup games allows them to test their partner's loyalty and dedication. It allows them to gauge their partner's willingness to fight for the relationship, ensuring they always have someone to cater to their needs.

4. Maintaining a False Self-Image

Narcissists often have a well-crafted false self-image that they project to others. By playing breakup games, they can manipulate the narrative and make their partner appear as the one who is at fault or responsible for the relationship issues. This helps maintain their image of being faultless and perfect in the eyes of others.

5. Emotional Manipulation and Punishment

Narcissists are known for their ability to manipulate and control others' emotions. They can subject their partner to emotional turmoil and confusion by playing breakup games. This serves as a form of punishment for any perceived wrongdoing or failure to meet their unrealistic expectations.

Ways Narcissist Slowly Destroy

Here are several key characteristics of narcissistic abuse:

1. Identity Theft: This serious violation of personal boundaries and privacy underscores a manipulative behavior often seen in narcissists. When the perpetrator is connected to the narcissist's family or acquaintances, it reflects a destructive intent to exert control and inflict harm.

2. Harassment and Intimidation: The timing of these incidents indicates a coordinated effort to destabilize the victim, serving as a tactic to instill fear, exert power, or punish during a vulnerable time.

3. Emotional and Psychological Manipulation: The chaos surrounding your personal information can create feelings of anxiety and helplessness, which is often the intended outcome. This leads to ongoing stress and a pervasive sense of unsafety.

4. Disregard for Your Well-Being: A complete lack of concern for the emotional toll that identity theft can take is emblematic of a narcissistic mindset, which prioritizes personal agendas over the well-being of others.

These actions disrupt not just your life but can also leave lasting psychological scars.

But it doesn't end there. Additional actions they take include:

1. Deception and Manipulation: Engaging in extramarital affairs and pawning significant personal items illustrates a profound pattern of deceit. This manipulation not only erodes trust but also highlights a lack of regard for the emotional impact on loved ones.

2. Lack of Empathy: The decision to pawn his wedding ring and other meaningful belongings reflects a significant disregard for the emotional significance those items held. A narcissist often prioritizes their own needs over the feelings of others.

3. Entitlement and Control: The financial transactions made to various women signal a sense of entitlement and a desire to control his narrative. Narcissists frequently believe they deserve to fulfill their desires, regardless of the consequences for those around them.

4. Addiction to Validation: Pursuing affairs and maintaining connections with multiple women point to an insatiable need for external validation. This behavior often stems from deep-seated insecurity, where the narcissist seeks affirmation to bolster their self-image.

5. Victim Mentality: Individuals with narcissistic traits often view themselves as victims of circumstance, justifying their harmful actions instead of taking accountability.

AFTERWORD

Thank you for joining me on this journey through *Till Betrayal Do Us Part: A Memoir of Surviving Narcissistic Abuse.* Crafting this memoir has been a deeply personal and transformative experience, and I am profoundly grateful for the opportunity to share my story with you.

Your support is invaluable to me, and I sincerely hope that the experiences and insights shared within these pages have resonated with you. My hope is that you find solace and strength in the knowledge that life can indeed flourish after experiencing the profound challenges of narcissistic abuse.

If my story has touched you, I would be deeply appreciative if you could leave a review on Amazon and Goodreads. Your feedback is crucial, not only in supporting my journey as an author but also in helping others find this book and its message of resilience and recovery. By sharing your thoughts, you contribute to spreading a message of hope and healing to those who may need it most.

Be sure to subscribe to my newsletter to stay informed about upcoming releases, special giveaways, and other exciting updates. Together, let's foster a community dedicated to reclaiming our true selves and finding strength in our shared experiences. Thank you once again for your support and for being a part of this journey. Thank you again for your support.

Cheryl Dyson-Bennett
www.cheryldysonbennett.info

You can also find me on:
Instagram
Facebook
Facebook Group

To further support you on your path, I invite you to explore the *Till Betrayal Do Us Part Study Guide*. This guide offers additional resources, discussion questions, and practical exercises designed to deepen your understanding and assist you in your healing journey. Whether you're reading alone or with a group, the study guide will provide valuable insights and tools to help you navigate your experiences.

You can find the
Till Betrayal Do Us Part Study Guide on Amazon.com

ABOUT THE AUTHOR

Dr. Cheryl Dyson-Bennett is a highly esteemed life coach, acclaimed author, and sought-after motivational speaker, dedicated to guiding individuals toward realizing their highest potential. As the visionary Chief Executive Officer of Designed for Greatness, LLC, and Women of Destiny Empowerment Enterprises, Cheryl leverages her extensive experience and passion for personal development to inspire transformative growth in others.

Cheryl's literary journey began with the release of her first book, *In the Arms of Jesus: Favor, Increase and Promotion*, in 2019, followed by the impactful *Divine Keys to Unlocking Your Destiny*. Since then, she has authored five additional books, each contributing to her mission of empowering and inspiring others. In addition to her books, Cheryl has created a plethora of journals designed to guide readers in their personal and spiritual growth, offering practical tools for reflection and self-discovery.

Her love for writing dates back to her childhood, when she would spend countless hours crafting stories and poems. Recognizing the profound power of her words to effect positive change, Cheryl pursued writing with a fervent dedication that has only deepened over time. Her works are infused with themes of hope, resilience, and divine guidance, drawing from her personal experiences and her unwavering belief in the power of faith and divine timing.

Cheryl's life mission is to empower women to navigate life's trials with grace and purpose, ultimately leading them to a fulfilling and purposeful existence. Her personal experiences with adversity have fortified her belief in the power of divine intervention and the importance of trusting in God's perfect timing. These challenges have not only strengthened her resolve but have also enriched her writing, making her messages of hope and transformation deeply impactful.

In addition to her roles as a life coach and author, Cheryl is a dynamic speaker who engages audiences with her heartfelt messages and practical wisdom. Her seminars and workshops have transformed the lives of many, equipping them with the tools and insights needed to overcome obstacles and seize opportunities.

Cheryl is also actively involved in various philanthropic initiatives, supporting causes related to women's empowerment and community development. Her commitment to giving back reflects her belief in the collective power of individuals to create positive change.

With an unwavering dedication to unlocking human potential, Dr. Cheryl Dyson-Bennett continues to inspire and uplift individuals, helping them navigate their journeys with confidence and purpose. Her work stands as a testament to the transformative power of faith, resilience, and the pursuit of greatness.

CHERYL DYSON-BENNETT'S PUBLICATIONS

In the Arms of Jesus: Favor, Increase, and Promotion
Divine Keys to Unlocking Your Destiny: A 30-Day Journey to Unlocking Your Destiny
Divine Keys to Letting Go: A Guide to Mastering and Unleashing the Greatness in You, Let Go, and Take Charge of Your Life
Jesus Loves Me
Illuminating Your Path with God's Word: A 52-Guided Devotional to Enlighten Your Journey through Daily Prayers and Confessions

Journals
Pray, Trust, Wait, and Repeat
Divine Keys to Letting Go Prayer Journal
Anointed and Appointed Prayer Journal
I Am Blessed and Highly Favored Journal
Phenomenal Woman Prayer Journal

Stay tuned for Cheryl's upcoming book, *Moving Past the Hurt: Reclaiming Your Identity in Christ.*

www.ingramcontent.com/pod-product-compliance
Lightning Source LLC
Chambersburg PA
CBHW070458100426
42743CB00010B/1668